FREEDOM FOR A DAY

WHAT IF YOU BELIEVED FOR JUST ONE DAY THAT EVERYTHING WOULD WORK OUT PERFECTLY?

By

James Goddard

IPG

Intermedia Publishing Group

FREEDOM FOR A DAY
WHAT IF YOU BELIEVED FOR JUST ONE DAY THAT EVERYTHING WOULD WORK OUT PERFECTLY?

Published by:
Intermedia Publishing Group, Inc.
P.O. Box 2825
Peoria, Arizona 85380
www.intermediapub.com

ISBN 978-1-935529-12-5

Printed in the United States of America by Epic Print Solutions

TABLE OF CONTENTS

PREFACE

In September of 2007, driving back from Cape Cod, I made some decisions about *The Secret*, *The Power of Positive Thinking*, *The Law of Attraction* and *The Power of Now*. I had just finished *The Secret* for at least the second time, and decided, instead of fighting it, I would open myself up to the possibilities by living and acting the way the book says you should. I also decided if I was to help and show others that this really works, I needed to document it and write my thoughts and feelings daily to see if there was a pattern that could be seen and used to help others.

After working hard for seven months to incorporate the teachings of so many into my life, I knew and felt I was to write another book at the same time. I had broken the teachings down into daily practices, and it was working. I was doing my normal Real Estate sales in a market that was down almost 25%, yet my sales were climbing. It was as if I was not participating in the down market that was reality. I was not allowing it to be my reality. The Secret was working.

I was having the realization by April of 2008 that the concept worked. I was not acknowledging the negatives that I had allowed into my life before. I instead worked hard each day to improve my skills to be a more upbeat and positive energy tower. Even though others, including myself, would say I am a very upbeat, positive person by nature, there was still much room for improvement. I realized I did not need to have my life be like the people around me (or society) thought. I could have my life and achievements be whatever I wanted.

It was then that I realized that if people would give the concepts behind *The Secret* and the works of so many other writers a chance, even for one day, it would work. If people would take just one day of their lives and live it to the fullest, believing that it can work. The negative does not need to be in your life. I wanted to show everyone that they actually invite in the negative and allow it to grow within their minds. What is around them is just an excuse the mind uses to support its negative behavior. Really, this was to show everyone how we unconsciously fall into patterned behavior each day. Unconscious behavior, and then we wonder why our lives are what they are!

I wanted to get people to give it all they have, for just one day. I mean, what is one day?

In May of 2008, combining the principles of many authors, I developed a program for myself that I felt would help me live *The Secret* to the fullest so I could truly write about it and help others. I was able to change the routine of my life that I would have argued was important and unchangeable.

When I woke up, sure I made the coffee first thing (no desire to change that part of the routine), but as it brewed, instead of getting my emails and going into my regular stuff, I sat down and wrote out 5 things I was grateful for. I would then head to the bathroom mirror and do my affirmations looking right into my own eyes (talk about feeling goofy at first). Then I would go read for about 10-15 minutes, some of

The Secret, Power of Now, Master Key System, or some other book. I can name about 6 good titles I read during this time period each day. I would then go into the living room and meditate for 5 to 15 minutes. I am A.D.H.D., so meditation was something my mind had convinced myself I was not able to do. I learned my mind had put many shackles on me without my knowledge.

For the entire month of May, I did this, along with keeping my thoughts and self talk under a microscope. I lived each day to the fullest, so that I could write this book during the month of June.

In Real Estate, June is one of the biggest months of the year. To dedicate time to write a book should be impossible. There was no question in my mind that I could do this. I started the book I know I was supposed to write on June 5th and at 6 a.m. on June 27th, I completed it, while sitting in front of the computer screen watching the sun rise over the trees out the window.

I then continued to write in my blog (which I look forward to having come out in book form as well) so others may see the patterns that can be helpful to improve one's own life. You can also read about self-imposed shackles we not only put on ourselves, but also keep securely on and protected.

I can come up with so many clichés that have far more importance here to myself than ever before, but instead I ask you to open your heart, mind, and soul to the goodness of the universe that is out there for the taking. It wants to be a part of you. You watch, if you open yourself up and allow yourself to receive it, you will find the universe is out there just waiting to instill goodness into those that will allow it!

Final note: Yes, the Real Estate market was down 22% in Hillsborough County in 2008 in terms of numbers of sales, and falling prices on top of that is supposed to mean my income should have been down at least 30%, if not more due to this falling price factor. By October 2008, I had surpassed my 2007 income. Bottom line: I believed in my program, lived *The Secret*, and the blog will one day be out to show my daily mindset and growth.

In the meantime, read this and allow yourself to have a day like this, or maybe more than one. You can apply this program to any area of your life. Read, believe and allow it to happen.

James Goddard

*Side Note: After you have read this and put the proper mental energy doing what others have taught and shown works, Live it for one day. Then please email me at Jim@ FreedomForaDay.com and share your story, so it can one day be part of a collection for all to read. Be a success story so others may grow due to your beliefs and mental efforts.

DEDICATED
TO
JAMES BUTTON

By not judging and giving he changed lives,
mine was one of them!

YOUR LIFE CAN GET BETTER
EVERY DAY IF YOU ALLOW IT

CHAPTER 1 - THE NIGHT BEFORE

I sit on the edge of the bed, my hand against my cheek, trying so hard to find the right direction. How do I make things better? I know there is beauty out there, but I am just not feeling it like I think I should. I want to feel the joy. I know it is around, but it feels like it always seems to avoid me. I get up, walk over to the window and look out. The grass needs mowing. I run my hand through my hair and walk back over to the bed. I look over to my wife's bed stand and see the book, *The Secret*. Ok, I read it. I want to feel it and believe it, but I just don't think they understand. They have things so good in life and then try to make it sound as if it was hard for them. I find myself shaking my head back and forth as I think about that. They don't really understand. I swing my legs up onto the bed, interlocking my fingers behind my head, even though I want to slump down. Ok, Lisa, you have told me "I should live it," "Give it a chance." I'm struggling with this because I really feel like it is all just pie in the sky, but I feel like I need to give it a chance…or better yet, maybe you could say I am at the point that I will try anything.

Tomorrow. Tomorrow, I will live it for a day. I figure I can try for at least that long. What do I have to lose? I lean over on my stomach, stretch my hand and fingers as far as I can and get the corner of the book. I pull it a few inches closer to the edge of her nightstand, grab it and lean back up against the pillow. I smile and stare at the cover. I'm not sure how long, but I was trying to feel it and figure out why this cover was so important to them. What the heck is this disk? Ahhh, it must be a seal. Yah, that's it, like a secret document from way back. Well, that's kind of neat, an encrypted secret message. It makes me feel special, like when I was a kid playing pirate. Ok, I'll play. You had pain, Rhonda Byrne (author of *The Secret*). I read it, I saw your movie, and you got it to go away. Hmmm, and you said it was easy and that it has been passed down through the generations. Alright, tomorrow it is. So let's get a quick overview of your writings, Miss Rhonda, and see what I should do. I flip open the book and start to thumb page for page until I hit the first summary. Yes, that is what I will do. I will read the summaries.

So what were those biggest points you were trying to tell us? Gratitude, we need to be grateful. Okay. Affirmations, sure I can do that. Read a little of *The Secret*. You know, just open it up and see what it is you were supposed to have read. You know, let the universe let me know what is most important. Ok, I'll go with it. Meditate. Get yourself in a quiet spot and let the universe connect. Believe. Believe that everything will work out no matter what. Believe it and it will. Alright, allow. Hmmm… allow. Allow the universe to work for you; don't get in its way. Self-talk. Make sure you have positive self-talk; do not let negative things slip you up, or if they do, realize it and shut it down as soon as possible. Okay, this one might be tough. Oops, not believing self-talk, strike one. I can do this. Good thing it starts tomorrow. I feel my whole face shift as I smile ear to ear not sure if I am laughing at what I am doing or the extreme to which I am willing to go to.

Shifters! I need shifters! If my mind does walk toward yucky thoughts, what are the warm wonderful things I have to bring it back? Wow! Now, isn't that just part of the problem? I can't think of anything. I'm not really doing this right... think, think, think. My daughter Marissa! She is the most wonderful thing in the world and loves me no matter what! Hey, I am feeling better already. A small amount, but I do have to acknowledge that there was a small amount of goodness for a second there. Oh man, do I want more of that! Ok, what's another? I lean back and feel disappointed, so hard to find one. It shouldn't be that way, but that is just how it feels right now. I sure do need this to work tomorrow. I feel my eyes swell a little. I know I am an intelligent person, but it seems that does not really matter. It is the patterned behavior of the collective human being, and I am human. I do truly want things to be better, and I am supposed to be the one in control of that. Come on Jim, think. The beach, I will think of seeing the sunrise at the beach. I love that so. Good, found another. I feel a little better armed now.

I scrunch down now and reach over to shut off the light, holding tight to *The Secret*, not wanting it to get away. I cuddle it like a child would a doll and think about how I will make sure I give this my all tomorrow, just 24 hours from the very beginning to the end! Then I drift off to sleep.

WALK AWAY FROM ROUTINE
TO FEEL AND LIVE LIFE

CHAPTER 2 - TIME TO GET UP

I'm feeling like I am floating and then softly landing upon a nice soft mattress. Ahhh, my legs spread out, I am coming to life. I turn my head ever so slightly, feeling the softness of the pillow, my head only on the side of it. I really only enjoy the corner for some reason. 4:45. Wow! I usually don't get up for another hour still. I think I will grab another hour of sleep and turn onto my back, flip the pillow over with little effort and settle back down to sleep with my head perfectly in the middle. As I close my eyes, I can hear the birds chirping. Oh yeah, today is to be a different day. I must start from this very moment. If the universe feels I am supposed to get up now, well, I guess I should go with it. I said I would. I lie there listening to the birds. Wow, they are beautiful to listen to. I bet they are telling happy stories and saying "good morning" to each other. I love the sounds of the birds; I smile to myself, as I feel I have already put some mental effort into *The Secret* twist to the start of my day.

I feel myself smiling, as I affirm that today is going to be the greatest day of my life. The Dalai Lama says human beings waste so many of the precious moments they have. Well, let's make the most of these moments then. Sliding off the side of the mattress, my feet hit the floor. Ok, a quick trip to the bathroom, and off to my coffee. Ahhh, I can taste it already. Going down the stairs, I stop at the mirror and focus the best I can and tell myself, "Jim, I love you." Just doing that makes me smile and giggle at myself. Making my way around the breakfast bar, I reach for the cabinet that has the coffee in it and swing it wide open. I take it down, open it and suddenly slow down. Now wait a minute. Each day I do this on autopilot. My same old routine: make the coffee and feed the dog. Today is not routine. I flip open the cover and place it on the counter, lean down and slowly inhale through my nose, a small, slow, deep breath. Oh man that smells good! You know what, this cup of coffee is going to be flippin' good I say to myself, and that smile creeps back in. I sure am glad this isn't being watched like *The Truman Show*; I wouldn't want that. I get the coffee turned on and head to the dog.

The bathroom is his home. He has a very spacious 5' by 8' room with such a nice window, and he is there to greet me as I swing the door open. As usual, I walk past him so I can get the food-into-the-dish routine done and move on. Oops, wait, I stop three steps in and look down. "Hey Buddy." I reach over, pat his head, and then make my way to the dog food. As I open the bag, I look up and am looking into the bathroom mirror; the smile widens. *I feel like Uncle Scrooge when he was going through his transformation from mean spirited to feeling life.* All I have to do is mess up my hair, but due to it being kept cropped short, I will not be pulling that impersonation off very well. Before I know it, the dog is at my feet looking up. Hmm, was I looking at my big grin for five seconds? Or was it 30? I was kinda enjoying the newfound craziness.

In the dish the food goes. Maybe I should give him a little extra today. Nah, this is fine. I place the food on the shelf and turn to go out; one step and I stop. He's looking at me. Does he always do that after I have given him food? Why is he looking at me? Is it because he just can't figure me out? Wait, I am going to do this today, the greatest ever. I am going to give this my all; I need to make sure that I observe Jim to the 9nth degree. He is looking at me saying thank you! He appreciates what I have done for him. He is grateful. I take that next step to head out; however, the next step never comes. Instead, I look down again and decide to really go out of character. "Life is too much of a routine," I say to myself; get one thing done so you can rush off to do the next one. Then tomorrow you can do the same stuff all over again. I reach a hand down and lower myself to the floor, knees bent, back against the wall. "Come here, Buddy." I tap the floor, "Let me pat you boy," and over he comes. Thirty seconds later, I get up. Wow, that was only 30 seconds, but that dog is so appreciative right now and feels loved. Why don't I do that all the time? It certainly is much better than just waiting for the darn coffee to be ready. I feel good; isn't that funny? I feel good. That was a powerful 30 seconds and he's just a silly dog.

Back to the kitchen and get that coffee cup out. Hazelnut creamer? You know what that stuff is, so yummy. I don't know how they went years without it. Someone is a genius, and I hope they reaped the benefits from it. Ahh, but of course they did. They at least have the satisfaction of knowing there is a whole part of the morning world that loves him/her. In the cup it goes, and I see the slightly yellow liquid on the bottom of the cup as I pour in the morning java. I smile, oh that looks good, and take that first sip. I feel it going all the way down, ooooh, and slowly make my way to the table.

So what's next?, I ask myself as I sit there and enjoy the next few sips. Gratitude. That's what we will do, as I reach across the table and grab a pen and small notebook. Hmm, I write a number one, circle it, and think for a second. What am I grateful for? I know, this cup of coffee and I write it in. Number two is written and the circle goes around it. I need five of them, so let's see, that soft warm bed! Now let's get three, hmmm, well the first two were pretty easy. I look around the room. Buddy, I almost scream in my mind, that silly dog. I am grateful for him and how he loves Jim, no matter what, every day. Now four, I guess I am grateful for this table and this house too. I have a great roof over my head. Five, wow that was easy. Taking a sip and feeling satisfaction, I smile again and feel muscles all along the side of my face. That's funny, wonder if I should write more or save some for tomorrow? Lisa, I am so grateful for that woman in my life, six. That car of mine, sure do like that, seven. Alright, that's good. Now what else am I supposed to do? I feel inside I have already accomplished so much and usually I am not even up yet.

Affirmations. Yeah, that's what I am supposed to do next. I scrunch up my face trying to think of how to do that, and what I want to affirm.

After enjoying the rest of the coffee and pondering this, I head back to the coffee pot. Back in that routine, the second cup. I pour it and start to go to the computer. Need to start my day off - I really should get my messages and figure out what

I need to prioritize. I set the cup down and wiggle the mouse to bring the computer to life. This actually slows me down for a second. Wow, talk about connected to the universe. At one point, someone believed, and has connected people in a way, that had never been done before in history. But wait a minute, *The Secret* says we are all connected, and you can connect with whatever you choose, so choose carefully. This stops me and I get up and head back into the bathroom. I turn on the brightest light of my two switch choices and plant my feet in front of the mirror. The smile creeps back as I smile and say, "Today will be one of the greatest days of my life," and "Everything will work out perfectly." Now I lean forward a little and stare at my own eyes, "I love you." The smile grows more, and I can almost feel a chemical reaction in my body on a slight scale. Wow, I do feel a little better and feel my thoughts start to float off. How many messages you figure I have? Then my eyes widen and the smile grows even more. Wow, that was incredible. There I was starting to feel great, and for some reason, I needed to offset that by crawling back into my routine. Even though I want to say, hey, this is real life. There is no reason for me not to feel great today.

Ok, Jim, work with me now. I started to feel great and I want those feelings to grow. I said I would allow that to happen today. I must say, it has been a little trickier than I thought it would be. Woo, woo, woo, be careful Jim, the self-talk, convince yourself this is going to be easy. I then say, "I believe I will be able to make huge strides on this today especially since I have already made such huge steps, with so little, so early in the morning." I turn and lean on the windowsill and stare out into the backyard. What a beautiful pool we have, and we have had so much fun in that, but man

I need to get the chemicals taken care of, and, and, why am I doing that? I look at the chairs. Lisa did such a great job picking those out. She has such a talent on that stuff. I am a lucky man, and I know we are going to have some great parties here this summer. I can see it already. Kind of funny, I have these good feelings that are flowing through my body that I have not realized before. Is it because I am usually off to the next thing I have to do, that I am not able to appreciate what the moment has to offer?

There was a tingling in my ankles and legs as I thought of these things. I have never realized that before. I wonder if that good feeling has tried to flow before, but I stopped it and did not allow it to happen.

Coming back to the table as I ponder this, I see *The Secret* on the counter and grab it on my way by. I have done my gratitudes and affirmations, and look, I have only been up 15-20 minutes. I started to climb this beautiful mountain that has great views all along the way, and as I continue with *The Secret* thought process, I can say what a wonderful trip it is going to be and a rather easy climb. Staring off into the other room, I am thinking how important it is to stop along the way and see and feel all that is around. Do not be so focused on getting to the top of the mountain that you forget about the beauty along the path.

On go the glasses and to page one I open. So what secret message does the universe feel is most important for me right now? Hmm, the grateful stuff. So, Bob Proctor (a contributing author in *The Secret*), you're supposed to talk to me on this. You tell me, if I am grateful for all I have, then more great things will come into my life during the day. Wait a minute; I think I have this figured out. If you stop and take time to be grateful for what you have, this is where your focus and energy will be. If you are focused on this, obviously you will see more and more. Eckhart Tolle (author of *Power of Now*), tries to have you stop and home into the moment, and when we do, there is so much to be grateful for, if we let ourselves. I read on and allow my mind to absorb versus repel this data. I figure I am an intelligent man, and if all these people are saying these things work, well doggone it, I am going to do what I can to join this kind of group. Why fight it? It makes no sense. However, I think the reason we fight it is in *The Master Key System*. Mr. Haanel (author of *The Master Key System*) says that whatever the conscious mind says (spoken word), the subconscious will support. You know, ever since I read that and meditated on it, it has been so easy to see how the human being is not in control of his responses so many times. I have heard people's extremely illogical responses and have not replied to them because I know they will just spit out another to try to support their spoken word.

I do have to say though, I have spoken to a couple of people the next day when they are not in the moment that they were trying to support the conscious and they are a little more open to hearing about themselves.

Meditation. Hmm, not sure about this one. I don't want to waste time; I want to make the most of it. Ouch, there I go again. You know, I just know I am going to connect so well and have such a perfect meditation. I know that the 10-15 minutes I use to meditate will be one of the greatest ways possible to start my day. It will help me focus so much and give me the clarity I really need to get the most out of this one day. I get up, and instead of thinking of all the things I usually do, I walk over and sit down on the floor. I can't really cross my legs, (I just have far too many muscles in them to be able to do that :)), so I just kind of cross them and put my back up against a chair. Ooooh, deeeeeeep breath, in and then slowly out the mouth. As I close my eyes, I look up at the clock: 5:43. Wow, time has flown, but I still have done so much. This is wild. In with the next breath and out. I hear a slight whistling in my head, kind of like a high-pitched squeal. I focus on it, and it gets louder and louder. Wow, that is cool; I forget about my breathing and just let my thoughts go.

Seven minutes and so many thoughts later, my eyes open. I am looking straight ahead at the clock. I put each hand out to my side, almost like I am steadying myself but not and it just feels good. I realize for about the fifth time this morning that I am smiling. I now get to my knees and get up with the help of the chair. Wow, that felt good. I head into the other room to the computer. Now I am going into my typical routine, but I do have to say I am doing it with a much different attitude. I feel good. I feel like I can't wait for Lisa to get up. I want to spend some time with her. I always love just the fact that she is right there. She doesn't have to say a word, or do anything, but if she is there, my heart feels good.

I sit down at the computer and wiggle the mouse. Ok, come to life, you silly box, and I sign in. As I do, I am thinking, you know, I am heading into my email with such a different attitude this morning. I am not going, oh man, what's going to be here. Instead, what person has connected with me? What surprise is here? I feel good on the inside, as my mouth is hanging open, and I feel the tingling moving from the middle of my face outward. Then I wonder. That darn piece of land that isn't selling. Are the sellers on here or is that one going to expire in the next month? Will I get a buyer? Feels like....

I stop. I have such a blank look on my face. I am so glad I am catching this all so early; that is quite a mental process I have going there. I was feeling great, smiling away, thought about all the good stuff that could be here, and then put an end to that. Why, why, why? Why did I insist that since I was feeling so good, I needed to offset it with some potential crap?

OK, refocus here. It is just for a day. I am going to take all that stuff and throw warm and fuzzy on it! Those sellers didn't email me, or if they did, it will be great to touch base with them; I have been wanting to. I just know that property will sell, it's just a matter of time. Probably in the next week or so, you watch. Somehow, magically, the smile has crept back in without me even realizing it. Just like the frown had taken over part of my face before. I shake my head in disbelief of what I was doing to myself and quickly realize that this also is wrong. I nod up and down. Instead of focusing on how I was messing up, I nod and compliment myself on how I had caught it. Good job, Jim!

After the typical emails, and the cool one or two also, I realize that I was responding with warmth and happiness. I decided that with each reply I wanted to put a touch of joy into each one's life. It felt so good that I decided that I would add a little something to my secret for a day. I am going to say something nice to the first five people I come in contact with. Yeah, let's try that and see how that goes.

I get up and look over at the clock. 6:15... I should let Lisa sleep a little bit more. I walk over and look at the books on the counter. *The Master Key System*. Okay, read that twice. Now, did I do a chapter a week like they say? Ahh, no. How about one a day? I read it either on the table here eating the morning cereal or the copy I printed out at work. Each morning, after all those emails and calls, I would put my feet up on the desk and absorb a little. Now, if I was going to use a little wisdom from Mr. Haanel here, what would it be? Ok, he says that you connect to the universe with your thoughts, now the universe is everything and anything. Ok, well it is like the subconscious connects with the universe, and that is how things appear or come to be in your life, but you connect to the subconscious with your conscious, or better stated, your words and thoughts. So you need to control your words and thoughts, and how do you do that? Discipline, that's how, silly. But how do you know if your thoughts are not pure and good?

By what you are saying or feeling, that's how. That is what he says: be mindful of your feelings. Your feelings tell you what you are thinking.

I sit and look out at the pool in the backyard. Wild, just plain wild, if I get this right, if I am not feeling good, it is because of what I am thinking. If I am not saying nice things, I am not properly connecting with the universe in the positive way I want to.

This is going to be a heck of a day, so I need to make sure I say nice things all day long. No joking, none of the "oh I was only kidding," not for today. Then, if I am not feeling up like I should be, I need to realize my thoughts have floated and say a few nice things to offset. You know, I can do this, and it might be pretty interesting how this day goes. Mr. Haanel, you are going to be stamped on Ol' Jim Goddard today, and I heard in my heart, *Give those extra seconds to those you love.*

GIVE EXTRA SECONDS TO THE
LOVED ONES IN YOUR LIFE

CHAPTER 3 - HONEY WAKE UP

I open the door and walk quietly into the bedroom, smiling as I see her sleeping so peacefully. She is beautiful, wonderful, and more than a man could ask for! I walk around to the side of the bed and remember she is the first one I am seeing, so I need to rain some golden wonderful words down upon her. I softly sit on the edge of the bed, and rub my hand across her back. Back and forth, back and forth, enjoying and appreciating how soft and smooth her skin is. Funny I see her take so much time and effort each day taking care of her skin and body, and right now I am realizing not only have I not slowed down to see, feel and appreciate it, but I have not acknowledged it to her either. Lost in my thought, I decide I need to make sure I let her know all the effort she has put into it has paid off incredibly, her skin is beautiful. You know I feel a little silly with this thought, but Lisa and I have had eight wonderful years together, and I have seen the efforts she puts into herself. Obviously, it is something important to her, and I have ignored it. Suddenly I see her eyes flutter, coming to life, breaking out of that dream world that we walk to each night. I smile as I watch the metamorphous take place. "Hey beautiful," I lean down closer to her and softly say, "you don't need any more beauty sleep, it isn't necessary." I gently kiss her shoulder and move my head to the side looking straight into her eyes and say, "You have such soft beautiful skin. I love how it feels," as I rub my hand across her back and watch her appreciation of the compliment start to take over her body.

I see the corners of her mouth start with a slight curl up, and the rest of her face becoming radiant. I keep rubbing her back, tell her I have coffee all ready for her downstairs, and how nice it would be to sit out on the back porch for a few minutes and enjoy a cup with her. I then lean down and gently kiss her face, and head off to my step-daughter Jamie's room to get her up. Each morning it is a mad scramble around the house with her and Elliot (my step-son), each getting up late and starting the day on a tired rush note, I open her door and reach out and touch her foot.

"Hey Jamie, you're not being very fair to all the other girls getting this much beauty sleep," and a reaction far more than I ever expected came to be. I do not watch her face slightly curl up like Lisa's did, but I watch it go wide, and her entire face is glowing. Wow, I think to myself, such a simple line, and I sure didn't expect that. Ok, two people, two nice things said, and I head up to the third floor to wake Elliot.

"Hey, buddy," I say as I walk in and see his face turned away toward the wall so I cannot see it. He has his hair cropped short right now; his Mom thinks he is so handsome no matter what, but she sure did love his long flowing hair. I do have to say though, he is one of the lucky guys who can pull off a great look with short or long hair.

"Dude, doesn't it feel so good sleeping on a nice soft bed

with this perfect sleeping weather?" Slowly his head comes around, and his face is smiling, as he is relating with the beauty of sleep not the fact that it has come to an end.

"Ya," he says, and pulls the covers up to his shoulders and tucks the top in around his neck. "It sure does."

"The Red Sox won." I didn't see the replay but did see that they had won on the computer, and off downstairs I go.

Wow, is all I can say to myself as I go. I thought this would be neat and a good way for me to start to get myself into a real nice frame of mind, and not only do I feel good, I feel I just got the universe around me off to a beautiful, wonderful start. They are now going to head out into the world with a far different mindset than they ever have before. I ask myself, why do I not have it begin this way every day? Why is it that I get caught up with routine, and do not take a moment to say something nice or get them to enjoy the right side of the bed as soon as they get up? Of course I know the little every day monster inside me wants to yell out, "'Cause there is real life out here, pal!" You know, bills to pay, work to do, and real life people that always want to rain on your parade. It is almost as if they feel it is their purpose in life. Nope, it is not that way today. I am not going to allow those thoughts to be a part of this day. Today I will believe and see to it that every thing works out perfectly.

Now my reflection goes back to the right here right now, and I ask myself, so how much extra time did all this take? Well, if I was to really calculate it all out, maybe 30 seconds.

I would have said a thing or two to Lisa to start any way, just would not have been the warm and fuzzy, and I really did not rub her back for long at all. Jamie, I spent no extra time with, maybe 5 seconds extra. Before, I would have gone in and it would have been a lot more like, "Hey, do you see what time it is? You have to get going." Elliot had no extra time. I know he will eventually get up; it is just a matter of him skipping breakfast because he had not gotten up early enough.

I get back down to the kitchen and there she is. "Ahhh, the woman of my dreams," I say. "Coffee smells good, doesn't it, Honey," as I grab my cup and put some of the yummy creamer in. Only enough for a half a cup, I don't really feel I need it, but to sip coffee on the back porch with her is a joyful thought. To heck with thinking all day how nice it will be to sit on the back porch with her tonight and enjoy a glass of wine. Why not start it here and now? And as I am walking to the porch, I am thinking to myself, why is it that I feel I need to do an entire day of what my inner self feels are things I need to do so that I can take time to enjoy the moment? I am shaking my head at the thought, thinking deeply of how I usually explain to Lisa at night all the things I did during the day, almost as if I am trying to convince her and myself that I have accomplished enough to be able to enjoy the moment.

I open the French door, and out she goes. I decide to leave it open and take the seat almost next to her. I see she is smiling, and inside, I am thinking how incredible it is that this has touched these guys. I was the one who was supposed to benefit, and I guess the way I benefit is by having the people around me light up my atmosphere, or universe you can say. I have made my home so much more pleasant this morning. Isn't that funny? Instead of focusing on some future point or event in which we could find some form of relaxation or positive feelings, we are living those feelings right here, right now.

So, Eckhart Tolle, this is what you are trying to say in *The Power of Now*: we do not live in our right here, right now world. Alternatively, if we are in it, we, meaning our minds, escape to some future point or event. Hmm…, I guess I am staying right here, right now. I normally go into all I need to get done today, how I don't have enough time and see how much more I should fit in. Then I focus on all I still was not able to do. I'm not going to think too much on that; Eckhart said you must constantly bring yourself back and be conscious of what your thoughts are doing.

Smiling and sipping the coffee, I hear Jamie coming down the stairs and then Elliot walks out to the table here on the screen porch and sits down. Kind of funny, he desires to be here with us; he feels the positive energy and wants to be part of it. He lowers his head and eats his cereal, but his face does not lean as far down into the bowl as it normally does; he is much more alive and awake this morning. I feel my insides smile with a sense of accomplishment. This was to all be for me, and they are the ones benefiting. I am a little wowed at this additional outcome that I had not expected, but I am able to see and appreciate it.

I look over at Lisa. "The birds sound beautiful this morning," and turn back as I see her close her eyes and take in the sounds of the morning.

Alright, I think it is time for me to slip into the routine part of my day; this has been wonderful, but I really should start making some more progress, even though I know I have all kinds of time. "So, Lisa, I would love to go to the gym this morning; you up for it?"

"Yeah, I would love to; what time you thinking?"

"Seems like if we get out of here around 7:15, it would be nice and relaxing. Does that work for you, Honey?"

"Yes, perfect."

I head up the stairs to get my ironing done, brush my teeth and get the whiskers off my face. Once in our room, I come to the ironing board, reach across to lift the shade, and the outside shines in. After turning on the iron, I walk to the bathroom to brush my teeth. I have the routine down so well: turn on the iron, brush and shave, then iron. Go eat and then either head out for my workout or hit the shower. This morning, I am not rushing through it though; I am relaxing into it, not worrying about what time I get to work. I figure I will get there when I get there. Everything will be there for me when I do, and it will work out perfectly, because it always does; I just haven't realized it before.

The kids left early today compared to usual, and I sit waiting for Lisa to come downstairs so we can head out to the gym. By the time she does, I am all relaxed sitting there, and she makes her cup of coffee to take with her. It seems to me she always tries to do just one more thing, and I have to try to exercise patience while she rushes around in hopes that I am not getting all tense. That is how the routine always works, but not this morning; today, I figure it will take her an extra minute at most, and today my day will be plentiful with time, and all that I want to accomplish I will be able to. Right now, I am in deep thought thinking of how I am part of the reason she rushes around. I am always off to the next thing, perhaps because I feel the need to accomplish more, more, more. I like people to look at all I have accomplished and have. Right at this moment, that is not feeling right. I feel as if I have rushed through precious moments and not lived life as beautifully as I possibly could have, because of a need to accomplish something to prove my worthiness or value. Slowing down so far today has allowed me to see what is around me. Today I feel I have gotten so much more out of the morning, yet the same amount of time has gone by. I have slowed down, but it is also as though I am the only thing that has slowed down. I so have to think about this more, I am thinking as Lisa's voice breaks my thought process.

"Sorry, Jim, I will be ready quickly," she says.

"Don't worry, Dude, I am so relaxed this morning, it's cool," I retort and get up from the chair and head to the door. I stand in the doorway to the garage and look at my vehicle. It is a 2007 Cadillac Escalade; now, how cool is that, huh? It is so beautiful and such a smooth ride, I am proud to own it and I have earned it. I place my hand on the hood as I make my way to the driver's side. Smiling, I tap the hood a few times and say aloud, "I appreciate you, car," and I climb in to wait for Lisa.

GIVE THOSE AROUND YOU
POSITIVE ENERGY, TIME, AND
ENJOY THE GIFTS YOU RECEIVE

CHAPTER 4 - THE GYM

Driving down the road, I feel so much more at ease than usual. I tell myself that I need to see, feel, and hear all that is around me; I need to connect with all that is out here, not just focus on a destination and get there as quickly as possible so I can do whatever I need to do so I can move on to the next thing.

I reach my hand across to Lisa. Funny, we used to hold hands all the time. Why do we not like we used to? We certainly do still love each other. Maybe we don't make the small moments all they can be. A little sad, isn't it? But right now, as I hold her hand, I see her face light up, because this has not happened for a while; when it does, it is because she is the one reaching her hand across. I rub my thumb across her hand as I drive and take in the scenery. I drive this road many times a day, but there are so many things I don't see. So what is it that I do see?

My mind starts to wander as I ask the question of myself and then I decide I want to think about this later, because right here, right now, I get to be with Lisa and I want to connect in every way possible. "So what are your plans today?" I ask.

"Oh, work on my cards," she says as she looks out the window and mentions that she wishes she brought her camera because she loves how the sun is shimmering off of something outside.

I smile. She works on her cards every day. This is her part of *The Secret*. She has been taking pictures and making cards for months now and feels she has hit upon a blockbuster concept; it has even become hard to get her to do housework, she is so focused. She is so inspired and passionate and wants to keep doing pictures and cards. The house has become Cardland with the downstairs computer room desk and the dining room table overflowing on to the floor. She is not "obsessed," that isn't a strong enough word.

"I got the Forgiveness Card online yesterday. I bought a whole separate website for it," she says.

"Oh, did you now? And how is it coming?" I ask as I look over at her smiling.

"What?" she says. "What are you smiling about?"

"I just love how you pour yourself into your cards, your whole mind, heart, and soul," I share with a smile.

Maybe I should step back a little; I feel it is important to share the background on this Forgiveness Card and concept. If you knew my wife, you would know that once she puts her mind to something, she is totally into it, there is no stopping her.

Down in Florida back in February, she captured the most beautiful picture of the sunrise, one so nice that you would think it fake. How could you possibly get the clouds to cooperate like that? It is as if the sky knew a picture was being taken that would touch millions of lives, that she was there for the purpose of taking that picture and just as she was about to snap the photo, a bird flew in because he wanted to be a part too (www.PayItForwardCards.com).

She made the photo into a card and has been working on the concept and wanting to get 3,000,000 of these cards out over the next 3 years. Each day, she works on it and when she talks about it, her face lights up and if she has a few extra moments, she is over at her desk putting the cards together. Almost every morning, sitting on the breakfast bar are envelopes she worked on the day before waiting to go out to some group.

She is smiling at me after my comment above and says, "Thanks. I just know this is going to be huge."

Into Hampshire Hills we pull; the ride seemed shorter this morning. I am normally focused on the destination, but today, I was relaxed and enjoying the ride. I look over at all the pansies they have planted; someone put a lot of effort into them and they look great.

I park and wait for Lisa to get her coffee cup situated. Once she does, we open our doors, both of us smiling like goofs; we really don't know why (although I'm starting to think I do). Another older man with a little hiccup in his step gets out of his car and his face goes to smile, as we both chime in, "Good morning."

"Morning," he says and adds to it after slight hesitation, "What a beautiful day!"

"It sure is and this workout is going to feel good today. You going to spank someone in tennis this morning, are you?" I ask as I see his racquet.

"You betcha," he says and although you can see he wants to keep chatting, we are heading inside and approaching the front desk. Should we have taken more time and properly introduced ourselves? Have I rushed here also? No, this worked perfectly I think quickly; there will be another day where we get to know him even more. This was simply a perfect first step!

"Good morning," we chime again and we see Christine light up.

"Good morning! How are you two today?" she asks as she is about to answer the phone.

"Great, thanks," we respond as we head down the hallway feeling like we are in a dream and what a wonderful dream it is. In hindsight, we saw the wonderful man in the parking lot, Christine at the front desk, and both added to the beauty of our day. At the same time, we added to theirs. It is almost as though we are batteries feeding off each other. The type of juice that our batteries provide is a warmth and goodness that connects with people that are on the same wavelength. My face scrunches a little as I suddenly realize that there were three other people sitting in the chairs that we walked

by. We didn't even see or connect with them today! I usually
see them and try to avoid the negative vibes they insist upon
giving off. They are always grumbling, I can tell you that.
They were there again today, but their negative energy did not
affect either one of us; they did not enter into our world, but
they were there. Wild!

I guess I will have to put that into my little thinking cap.
Imagine, today their desire to just exist, moan, or play their
pity party was not acknowledged. I wonder if I can do that with
other crowds. I wonder if I can connect with only what I want
to connect with. What if what I am giving off is what I will
connect with? If I give off poor-me vibes, I would see and be
attracted to others giving off similar vibes. I need to make sure
I control these emotions and feelings of mine and keep them
focused on the good stuff. So far, I have to say I like how I have
taken the good feelings and built upon them all morning. I have
not decided that I've had enough and should get back to "real
life." I am keeping this thing going. I go through the door and
look at the clock: 7:37. Wow, it feels like I have done so much
today, and I feel so relaxed and good. This is funny. I must keep
the good thoughts going. This is going to be a wild day.

After taking in the clock, I scan the room. I usually head
to the first piece of equipment like a robot and try to get as
much of a workout in as possible without making much contact
with anyone here. Got to get this workout in so I can race to
the next thing I have to do, so that someday in the future I can
relax. This feels like a very funny concept right now; I feel like
a cartoon character taking a sledgehammer to my own head
with this realization that does not feel like it is in the proper
perspective of life right this minute. If I were to give up on this

mental discipline of today, I would slip back and give great value to my regular way of life unconsciously. Not only that, I would argue it and not be open to hearing the potential of how wrong that line of thought is. I might even go as far as allowing my Ego to come up with reasons that you are a jerk and unworthy of telling me anything.

Instead of feeling poorly at the thought of having actually treated people that way, I instead think of how grateful I am that I have this awareness right now and can change and grow. I feel my head tilt to the side a little as I think of a belief that has been hammered into people: there is pain in change. I think it was the Ego and the Painbody inside of us that got together, had a meeting, and said okay, how can we get these silly human bodies to do whatever we want? One of their ideas was to make us believe there is pain in change, therefore, we will continue in the same unconscious patterned behavior we always have. Not only that, but we have taught ourselves all these supporting lines to use in case some other human being that has perhaps attained enlightenment tries to tell us otherwise.

"Good morning, Kathy," I say, as I walk past her coming up to the weights. "Great day, huh?" I look in the mirror to see my smile and look at her.

"Good morning! How's that daughter of yours? She get her internship yet?"

I feel my heart warm at the thought of Cassi. I had not even thought of her yet, but now that she has entered into my day, I realize I have another thing that always makes me feel so good. The unconditional love I have for that child is really something. I have always been so proud to know I am the father of that girl. She is 20-years-old now and doing her final internship for college, the New England Culinary Institute in Vermont. She is into her baking. It's like taking a fish and throwing it into the water. I have often wondered, was it because we would go pick berries or apples or you name it and I would have her up on the counter with me when she was a child and we would cook and bake together? I always viewed cooking and baking with such joy. I'm not sure if it is because I was so proud to have food to be able to provide, or whether I wanted to make it the best I could for the ones I love with what we had. I don't know. It's probably a bunch of those things together.

"Yes, she just got a job at a bakery down in Worcester with two of her college friends so she is in seventh heaven right now. The pressure has now turned to joy," I say with my face lit up.

"Oh, good, I am so glad to hear that," and I can tell she wants to keep talking, but we are both starting routines (she has been there for a while walking and is all sweaty) and she turns and walks to the next item on her agenda.

I reach down and grab the 65-pound weight. I turn to see which bench will be open. There are three of them behind me, only one I really like. It is straight all the way across without a bump in it where you can elevate your head. Today I just know it will be open for me.

Oh yes, how did I know? Did I will it? I am usually afraid

that it will not be available, that it will be taken, but today is a different day. Today everything is going to work out perfectly. I turn and plant my butt on the seat and look in the mirror straight ahead. Once again I see Kathy on the far wall, and I smile bigger. Then I see Russell lost in his thoughts as he looks at his clipboard; he does a great job at staying with his routine each day. I like the scattered approach myself, I *feel* like doing this today rather than the I *have* to do this today approach.

I lay down and start my first exercise. I focus on the weight as it goes over my head. I count as I move it over the end of the bench and back up over my head. Work those triceps. Two, three, and suddenly I realize I am far more focused on the action I am doing and feeling all the muscles in my arms that this exercise is touching upon. Why have I never felt them before? Then I realize it is because I am usually so focused on completing the number of repetitions and getting over to the next piece of equipment. Four, five, six. Wow, feels good. I can feel my muscles doing their job and growing.

I sit up and look at myself in the mirror. This time, I see my furrowed brow. I am going back in my mind. For ten plus years I have come here, and not once do I remember feeling my arms growing. I just head off to the next piece and watch the clock to see how long it is taking me and think what I am going to do after this. Now that I am living *The Secret* for a day, I realize what a wonderful breakthrough I have just made and how much more I am going to get out of lifting in the future.

Twenty-five minutes later, I am smiling over at Lisa. "You

ready?" she asks.

"Yeah, if you are set; if you need a little more time, I can go get a small run in."

"I'm good," she says, and puts her file away (another Russell type).

I hold the door open for her and smile back at Kathy. "Have a great day," I say as I slowly start my walk down the hallway with the one I love. "How was your workout?"

"Good," she says and then she goes into how she put the incline higher and starts telling me the stuff she usually does.

I normally throw in a "cool" and then tell her about mine, when it hits me: I need to let her know I genuinely want to know. We ask questions all day long that we really aren't looking for the answers to. I love this woman and I have treated her the same way, but I will now reframe the statement. I am so glad I know this now so I can show her more fully how much I care.

"So you ran how long at what grade?" I turn and ask her, and off she goes. Oh my goodness, she is erupting with data now, she is sharing stuff like you would not believe, and you can see how good she feels about herself for what she accomplished.

"Wow, you did really well today. I bet you look forward to the next time to see if you can expand upon that," and I reach over and grab her hand as we walk down the hall toward the front door.

I see a couple of people sitting in the chairs and I realize as they look at us, they may think our warmth is phony or never going to last. I wonder if that is just another one of the ways our mind tries to keep us in check and not waste our time being as nice as we can be. Why does it take mental effort to be compassionate? Shouldn't that be one of the easiest emotions to ever happen? I open the door for Lisa and have no answers for that right now – just confusion.

We step into the sunlight outside and I look up and think that maybe the best thing I can do is focus on all the beauty that is in and around me so that others may do the same thing. Perhaps the more positive light towers we have in this world the better. It certainly can't hurt anything, I think as I know I have my goofy smile back.

NOTES

Gratitudes

    1)

    2)

    3)

    4)

    5)

Affirmations

    1)

    2)

    3)

    4)

    5)

EVERYTHING YOU HAVE,
YOU ATTRACTED

CHAPTER 5 - BACK HOME

I have to slow myself down for a moment. Wild! Now think of that: slow myself down. Usually I would be freaking out that I had to get into work. I have things I have to get done, and I haven't done a damn thing yet. I slow because it is like a fog is melting away; I feel better this morning than I have in a long time, and I certainly have not had a work accomplishment. I go in the house and out onto the back screen porch to sit, letting myself really melt into the chair so my butt cheeks are barely holding onto the seat; I reach my feet out and put them up on the chair facing me. My arms are up higher than most of my body, almost resting on the arms of the chair. Now I look up at the ceiling and focus on the boards, but don't really see them.

When is the last time I spent a few extra minutes that were not part of my routine with Lisa? I am not delving into the negative here, but focusing more on how my heart feels so good this morning, and I am really only 15 minutes off my normal schedule. There really is no set time that I have to get into the office. Yes, it is true that I am pretty much the first one there each day, yet no matter what time I get there I feel like I am late. I have even learned to take an efficient shower where I have washed my entire body in less than 2 minutes to squeeze a little time there, too.

"Hey, honey," I yell out not wanting to leave my position. "Dude," I yell out again, as I did not realize she was in the bathroom and did not hear.

She comes into the kitchen (the layout goes kitchen/ dining area/family room and the French Doors go from the family room to the screened-in porch), "Where are you?" she asks from the kitchen, not knowing where my voice had come from, as this is certainly not part of my normal routine.

"Out on the screen porch. You going to have another cup of coffee?" I ask.

She walks over to the door and looks out smiling at me, "I was going to make a shake; you want one?"

"No, thanks," I say, my typical response. She puts such effort and care into her blended drinks. "Wait, yes, I would, but not a whole one. Just make it so I have a nice glass," I say smiling again and thinking of how good it is going to be. They always are or at least look that way. I just don't take the time to try or enjoy them like she does.

Suddenly I get up, almost falling off the chair due to my position, pop my head in the door and take a half a step in, "You want any help with it, honey?"

"Sure, can you get the fruit out of the freezer for me?" she asks.

I don't answer, but head for the freezer door, feeling all funny inside. Time is such a simple thing and what we crave, but we are not willing to give it away. If you are able to focus and stay in the here and now, it is not such a big deal. I would normally be attacking myself right now, saying I need to get this done, or that done, etc., etc. Then at the end of the day, I would get off of the hamster wheel and head off into the next part of the "gotta-do" stuff. There are so many things I decide are far more important than what really should be important. I might have to admit that I am a tad off my normal process. I could sit back and argue with you and give you all kinds of supporting reasons as to why my normal insanity is important; I could give you the "you don't understand," and "If you had my life, you'd know" lines. But today I have no desire to support that premise; what I realize right now is that my premise was incorrect, and I am thankful that I am able to see it as clearly as I can right now.

Think about it. You always think how life would be different if you had someone else's life, but what are they doing but making those same statements. I almost want to lean forward and bonk my head on the fridge, but instead my smile just grows. So far I have to say that forcing myself to relax, and stay "in the now" has been very healthy for me. I feel great, the people in my life feel great, and I am not spending my time worrying about all the worries I can usually create. Yet I feel I have radically reduced the chance of the yucky things happening; I am not giving them any value today, so I am therefore not allowing them into my universe.

People are usually sad and upset when they lose money or possessions, yet they give away the precious moments of each and every day with no remorse. That seems wrong right now. As a matter of fact, if I had the 70-year-old Jim come back and sit and chat with me, what do you think he would tell me? "Go out there, Jim; get more money. To hell with the kids and the wife, go make something of yourself"?

No, I don't believe he would say that. I feel he would say, "Slow down. Relax. Take time to see, feel and connect with all that is around you. You will always either have enough time or you will always not have enough time. Whichever you decide, Jim, will be right."

Once again I feel like a cartoon character; I feel as though my head is out of shape and I need to shake it vigorously for it to go back into its normal shape. Wow, floated off there, but I do feel like the float had value. I am going to freak out, I am thinking. Is it possible that this is my last day on earth, and this is what it feels like? You feel all the more, and everything has so much deeper value.

I reach out and touch Lisa's shoulder, as she is turning to look for the frozen fruit. I look right into her eyes with a rather queer look, "Dude, I love you," I say as I hesitate and hand her the fruit. "I am so glad you are in my life."

I almost expect an odd look, but for some reason she can feel and see the genuine way in which I mean it. "Thanks honey," she responds and she leans over to kiss me, smiling and looking straight into my eyes before she turns to put the fruit in the blender.

Sitting on the stool, I watch the pride she takes. After a

minute or two, I am handed a drink that looks wonderful, and I take a small sip. "Oh, man, this is gonna be real good," I say as I look up, eyes wide, and I move back to the porch. I don't have to turn to see that her face lit up with pride; I can feel it on the back of my neck. As I turn the corner to go back on to the screen porch, I do peek and see that as she is wiping off a little that spilled over on the counter, and she is lit up. She appears a bit lighter on her feet.

I stop and look at her. It is as though she senses what I am about to say, and she chirps, "I'm coming. I will be right out. I just want to get this up now so it doesn't get all sticky."

Perhaps she was responding to what I normally might have said. Okay, who am I fooling? Of course that is what I normally would have said. Today, I was seeing her, really taking her in, and enjoying the twist I have put into her day and my own, and I didn't feel a need to say anything.

After sitting for a few minutes, she finally asks the questions, "Do you have a long day today? Shouldn't you be getting into the office?"

I lean over after a sip of my shake, a big smile on my face, and give an abnormal response after a long hesitation, "No, not a long one today. I have plenty to do, but it will get done."

The smile gets even bigger as I am wowed by how my day has gone; I think I could call it quits right now and feel that this day was an incredible success. My eyes shift back over to her, as she is looking at me with a quizzical smile, "Maybe

I should get in, but it seems like such a nice morning. It has been wonderful just relaxing." Turning my gaze to the house next door, I start again, "I just know that when I get in, all will be perfect, so why rush? It always turns out perfectly, and Lori is there to take care of any real issue."

Now she is considering getting out a strait jacket, I am sure, wondering if I am safe to be around. Am I one of those cases you read about now and then where someone just snapped? I am the guy who rushes to get to the next thing all the time. It does not matter what it is. I say I enjoy something and I'm relaxed, but all of a sudden I am ready to move on. Right now is one of those times we always talk about and dream of. Yet it seems that the only time I am this relaxed is on vacation. Lisa finally has the seeds to ask straight out. She is getting freaked.

"You okay, Jim?" she asks.

"Yeah," I respond, staring straight ahead and furrowing my brow and thinking deeply. "I decided to put some of my readings to use today. I thought instead of running around and pounding through my routine, I would relax and believe that all would work out perfectly today no matter what. You know the adage, nothing is good or bad; it is what you make of it. Well, I decided that today I would make anything and everything good, no matter what. Gosh, am I getting into it today? Never have I been so relaxed. Although, I do have to say that on the inside, I keep getting this slight queasy feeling. I have to snub it right away and go back to good thoughts."

Turning toward her, I look right into her eyes. "Think about it, 99% of the population is rushing around today. Why?

There is so much beauty out there, and they will not take the time to see it. Why? Why? Why? I wanted to, for just one day, go about believing that everything will be perfect, and not allow anything to alter that." My smile starts to grow again. "Now, think about it. Why would this be a bother to anyone? Why should I not try it for just one day?"

"Today, I am not a part of the rat race. I am James Goddard, Mr. Relaxed, and nothing can change that today. Nothing. I will not let it. The issues, worries, and concerns we usually need to take care of are things we have created in our own minds. We decided they are important, but why do we do this to ourselves? I am going to break this down to the basics right now. That bowl of cereal this morning, I was really thankful for it, but how often am I appreciative of something so many do not get to have? Let's chat about that nice warm bed, or the good sleep I got, or the nice vehicle we have to go to the gym in. There are so many things we have that we overlook each day. The kids are healthy, and so are we. Check this out: my arms and legs," as I swing them both with a goofy smile, "they work perfectly."

"Lisa, this has been a really cool morning for me so far. Usually when you ask me if I want some shake, my mind defaults to no, but instead, today I imagined how good it would taste, and it did!" Smiling widely and looking directly into her eyes, "Thank you so much for making it. I really appreciate it; it was truly nice of you."

"Well, you are welcome. This seems like a neat idea; I think I will try to do the same thing," she says.

My mind automatically wants to say try means fail, but today I think harder, and instead of allowing my automatic response to occur, I think on this for a second. This is where I need to think about what I am about to say. I need to be my own scientific study all day. Suddenly I smile, because I stopped myself.

"I just know that you will do a great job with it. You are so naturally upbeat, anyway, it will be easy for you." I nod my head a few times as I take my gaze back to the bird that has flown up to the top of the roof next door. "And I am happy for all those you will come in contact with today; they are very lucky to be able to be touched by you. You know what?" I ask.

"What?" she says with a smile on her face. It is a thinking smile; you can tell she is part here and part not. She has floated off into her day and how she is going to do this.

"I have to get ready for work! I mean, I choose to get ready for work now; it is time to take this to the rest of the world." As I get up from the chair and walk over and plant a warm kiss on her lips. I didn't give a normal peck like usual. I stayed in it for the extra half of a second and looked into her eyes, smiling and saying I love you without ever saying a word.

I turn and bring my cup in to place it on the counter before heading upstairs, leaving her sitting in the chair, knowing that she is really taking this all in.

PEOPLE YOU WILL SAY NICE
THINGS TO TODAY

1)

2)

3)

4)

5)

ENJOY THE JOURNEY
AND SEE THE BEAUTY
YOU PASS EACH DAY

CHAPTER 6 - GOING TO WORK NOW

I took a much longer shower than usual. I even sat on the bench they built into our stand up shower. Imagine, they built it for someone to get the joy of sitting and just letting the water rain down. I ask myself, why have I not enjoyed that before? The only time I can say I have is when I had a little more wine than I should have the night before, and I need to sit to get my head together. During those times I do because I need to. It's very silly that I would only move toward joy in order to try to take the edge off. I do not believe that is what they had in mind when they created that bench. I feel they thought of how someone could enjoy that each day, or now and then, and not just for survival purposes. Oh well, I look up shaking my head a little, but still able to maintain my goofy smile. From this point forward, I will allow myself more joy. Instead of beating myself up once again for not enjoying life and trying to figure out why I would not allow myself joy, I am just going to vow that I will from now on.

Turning to go, I scan the room. What a beautiful room! We have so many wonderful things. I start to think of the joy each item gave us, why we have them on our walls or in the room here, and decide to carry on. I think I will take time during the ride in and dwell upon that, do a little gratitude again, and I head down stairs.

Where's Waldo? I think as I walk down the hallway into the kitchen seeking out the love of my life. As I come into kitchen and up to the breakfast bar, she gives me the school teacher look, peering at me over her glasses, yet keeping her head mostly down.

"I was thinking of actually going into work today," I say while smiling ear to ear and looking up at the clock. It is 8:43. I would normally be freaking out, but I do not allow any of those thoughts into my head this morning. Instead, I keep letting myself know that everything is going to go perfectly today. It is only one day. How can one not try to play the game for one day?

I walk around the breakfast bar and unplug my cell phone. Wow, I haven't changed my message yet. I am the greatest message changer in the whole world. Each morning in my message, I say the day so anyone who calls in will know I am up and working already. If I have some morning appointment and for some strange reason will not be able to get back to someone within minutes, I leave a message letting anyone who calls know that I am in a seminar or something. I mean, come on now, I work all the time. That is what I need to let everyone think. Not for a moment do I want them to think they are not the most important thing in my life. And for the first time ever, I think about this a little more. For the first time ever, I am not sure my thought process is proper.

I shake my head. Not today. Today I do not need to figure this one out, I think as I walk over to Lisa and lean down, puckering my lips with my eyes squinty from smiling so much. "Kiss me, baby," I request, looking at her and watching her lean her head back. "I was thinking maybe we should have lunch today."

Now in my mind, funniness was setting in, but I feel this is where I need to keep an eye on self. I wanted to say jokingly, "If you think you can fit me in." That is a typical Jim statement. Always joking. But what if, on the inside, I was thinking more of how nice it would be to connect with her during my day, how it would give me something to look forward to all morning. I would not usually offer that up because it would take away an hour of work time. If *I* grab something quickly, I can eat and work at the same time. Do you realize how much more I can get done each week eating by myself?

I wander back into today. It's just one day. Looking down at her, I say what I feel: "Honey, it would make my whole day to be able to have lunch with you. Can we please?"

I see her figuring things out in her mind; she is a planner so I get to hear all the things that she is going to be doing today, knowing that eventually she will make her decision. Eventually she starts to nod her head a little, "Yes I think I can. What time were you thinking?"

"Whatever works best for you. I can do an early one or a late one," and I start toward the door while looking back at her.

"I'll give you a call or send you an email. I will see how much I get done and how things are going," she says.

"Great. I look forward to it. See you soon," and out the door I go.

It is only a 10 minute drive to the office, a perfect amount of time to call in get my messages and get things in order as to what I should do first when I arrive; however, I want to do a refresher first today. This has worked so well, and it would be so easy to finish right here, right now. (Oops, wrong stuff to put in the universe.) I am getting so much joy from this so far this morning that I want to go deeper and get even better. I decide that I am going to start my gratitudes all over again.

Driving down the road, it seems a little weird. I am doing just a few miles over the speed limit. Usually I push it right to 9 to 10 miles per hour over because I figure that is the most you can get away with; instead, I am chilling and in a relaxed manner going over in my mind the next gratitudes.

I am so grateful for this Cadillac. So sweet, so smooth a ride, oh yes, this is really something to be grateful for, smiling big again. And my eyes. With them I can see all the trees and flowers as I drive down this street. I look down at the drink holder and grab the water bottle. I always have waters in my car. I am grateful for this water and this sharp looking suit. Okay, one more. Where can I find another one? I look in my rearview mirror and on the seat next to me. Geez, I can't think of anything, so I just go into my affirmations.

Looking in the mirror as I drive, I am still smiling, and I let myself have it: "My life gets better and better every day."

I look away and make sure I am on the road; even though

I'm only going 35, I still need to stay safe. Looking back up again, I say to myself with great satisfaction, "I love you, Jim, you're a good person." I then look straight ahead and concentrate on the road. Wow, I sure am doing a good job with this; now I need to make sure I say nice things to those I come in contact with. I pick up my phone and start to dial the backdoor line to the office to get my messages. But I freeze. Wait, Jim. Not yet, no messages yet. I turn on the radio and decide I am going to relax all the way in. It shouldn't be a big deal, it's 4 more minutes at the most.

I listen to the music and enjoy. I start to float off. Usually, okay not usually, almost every day, I get behind a slowpoke and end up wondering, "Why me?" Today, I look in my rearview mirror and see that a car is catching up to me; now, that is rare. So where are the slowpokes today? Is it National Slowpoke Stay Inside day? Then it hits me. Each day I race until I catch up to the next car, and once I finally pass, I end up catching up to another. It is not a conspiracy against Jim; I am the one creating this pattern. Or as the readings say, I attract it. Each time Lisa points out that I do this I have to bite my tongue; right now, I wish she were here so I could tell her. Maybe I will tell her at lunch… or maybe not, I smile to myself, not wanting to give her *that* much satisfaction.

The clock reads 9:02 as I pull into the office parking lot, and a great song is playing. It is Allan Parson's "Eye in the Sky," and instead of the turning off the car and heading into work, I park, lean back, crank the tunes and enjoy.

Now, here comes the strange part. One of my co-workers (she has to be in her mid sixties at least… probably closer to

70 - gosh if she isn't, sorry, Ingrid), who is the number two agent in the office, a real producer and a nice woman, parks her car almost next to mine, and walks around to my driver's door. With a slight hesitation in her walk, she suddenly looks over at me, smiles and gives me a thumbs up. Wow, I didn't expect that, Ingrid. It was as if she could see, feel, and sense the relaxation and beauty I was receiving from the song.

As the song ends, I feel good. It is a few minutes after nine. I go to take my keys out, and what do you know, another awesome tune comes on! I smile to myself, and shake my head. "No, Jim," I end up saying out loud and I climb out of the car. It's about 25 steps to the entrance of the office, but I stop after about 15 of them to look back at my car. Why? Why did I not stay and listen to that song? I nod my head. I know why - I need to get to work eventually, so it is time. Nevertheless, I still think more deeply on it. For "Dream Weaver" to come on right after "Eye in the Sky," it is almost as if the universe saw how much delight I was getting from the music and decided to send me another beauty, but I did not allow myself to partake. I wonder if the universe is a little sad. I did say I would allow myself the beauty of the day all day, and I just walked away from one. Inside I quell the feelings of "Dude, you need to get to flipping work."

As I go to open the door, I look at the huge PJM Rhododendron in full bloom and say wow to myself. Usually, when I hit this point I look down at the butts that Mike has thrown on the ground and bum out because it smells like smoke out here. Now that is something to think about. Why is it that I choose to see the grunge and not the beauty that nature has provided? I am sure there are other areas of my life and day I need to be more aware of. However, I put my Secret twist to it and I say out loud as I come through the door, "Today is the day that I see the beauty. I am so lucky that this is what my eyes and ears will pick up all day today."

Now I flow into routine. I need to make sure I give it a bump or two as I go. Sign in, check my inbox for mail, turn and instead of head down reading as I head to the third floor, I look up at the other human beings in my presence. I am usually respectful, but none of these guys is going to buy a house from me and I am here to list and sell, so I usually head right upstairs. Ingrid looks up at me and very stoically inquires, "Good song? You looked like you were really enjoying it."

"I sure was. Great song just happened to come on as I drove in; normally I would just shut it off and start my day, but today I decided to relax and enjoy," I respond, smiling big while thinking of myself sitting there with the cranked tunes.

Then she goes into some story about her daughter and some concert or something like that (I should apologize to her for not taking more time and listening to her). It was nice that she shared; it is her nature to keep to herself, so it felt good that she was opening up.

Turning to go, I stop myself again and step into Sandy's office. Smiling I say, "Ol' Dice K pitched pretty good last night, huh? The Sox are looking good so far this year."

She looks up, and she does have quite a grin; I never really focused on it much before, but I do know that if you throw some sort of sports thing out, you can easily get her attention and connect. "Yes, he did, didn't he? They are pulling it together real nice. I thought maybe their pitching would give them trouble this year, but they are doing well. I didn't watch the whole game though. I went to bed around 10, just after they pulled him out and brought in Timlin."

"This feels like it will be their year again. It is a fun time in history to be a Red Sox fan." Then I head out to get to my office.

Going up the stairs, I feel so different today. I am starting to get the feel that life is cool, life is wonderful, and although it is a day like any other day, I decided it was to be different. I am the only factor that has changed; however, that appears to have changed all that is around me. I have changed my own little universe. I have made it better so far today simply with altering how I approach things and through the focus and energy I am giving off.

I make the final few steps into the penthouse suite (or the top floor that is too cold in the winter and too hot in the summer, but to Lori and me, it is the penthouse suite). I come around the corner and Lori has turned to look at me; she is smiling a sly smile and says, "About time you decided to come to work, slacker."

She knows this is funny because of how much I work and how much I dedicate myself. I rest my butt against the third desk in our office and say, "You have no idea what my day has been today."

To give you background on Lori: I have preached *The*

Secret to her, and not only that, I told her that she could read it on my time. I felt that if I surrounded myself with more positive energy, it would create more of it. She has heard me speak on it for over seven months now, and she is so into it when I speak on it. I shared with her that we were going to approach real estate differently this year, and that we needed to be very careful with our self talk and how we approach things. Together we can do so much more.

My thought process was this: Imagine the amount of energy that an individual can put toward a certain goal. Well, if you have two or more people putting energy toward a common goal, it could quite possibly be something spectacular.

We have talked about this many a time, and some of the examples we usually come up with include Tom Brady and coach Bill Bellichek of the New England Patriots. Think of it: they believe so strongly that the others around them believe. Remember the Super Bowl they just lost? It was the defense that was on the field, not the offense. The offense had just scored a touchdown and the defense actually missed a few plays that would have sealed the victory. The universe was there for the Giants. You need to respect that and even if you do not care for Eli Manning, that man was not going to allow defeat. There was an energy field around the Giants that would not allow defeat that day. My theory is that it was actually given off by Mike Strahan. I hope to be able to sit and talk with him about it one day.

"Okay, Lori, listen to this, and you need to help me. I decided that today I would do things differently for just one day. I decided to live *The Secret* for just one day and see how it goes, and this has been a wild day to say the least." I realize that my eyes are wide and my smile huge as I go over my game plan with her and tell her about how my morning has gone so far.

"So today, I need you to think only positive, wonderful, perfect endings on everything, so that we create only that energy. I want to make sure that for just this one day, I give it all I have and then tomorrow…" I hesitate as I think about tomorrow and as my face goes into a thinking look, I turn it right back into my grin. "Well, we don't have to worry about tomorrow. We have right here right now to give this all we've got." I look at her and see that she is nodding her head up and down. "So you with me, buddy?"

"Sure, it sounds like a good idea."

"You mean a great idea, huh?" I prompt, smiling big. "Now tell me something good."

She goes into a story about her newborn, Levi, about how he smiled at her and snuggled into her arms last night and feel asleep so peacefully, and instead of my usual smile and one word acknowledgement, I smile and go a little deeper to say, "Wow that must have made you feel so good, huh? He is really a little lovebug, isn't he?"

Now the response that I knew I would get, I got. It is as if I just wound up a toy to the max and set it on the floor: she is off and going. This obviously made her feel good, and she wants more of those feelings so she is sharing more and more and more. I am smiling and nodding all through this.

I feel I have given a small amount of time to so many, why would I not also do that for this wonderful person?

DON'T LET YOU,
GET IN YOUR WAY

CHAPTER 7 - THE WORK ROUTINE

I walk over to my desk and stand there for a second. Usually I have five different things I try to do at once. Stuff on the top of the desk. Emails, check expires, phone messages, what do I do first? I normally feel a bit of panic because each segment has its priorities and things that need to be done. Or is it that my mind creates that line of thought in the hurry to move on to the next task? This is the first day that I am looking at things with a different eye. I simply take a deep cleansing breath and sit down.

I reach over and grab the papers on my right. I feel I should clear my desktop as much as possible first. All the other things will have their time. I should not have left these open-ended tasks. In a more relaxed manner than usual, I take out my Post-Its and start to write out the task that is associated with each paper to put it on Lori's desk, when my smile starts to grow again.

Looking down, I notice that I can easily read everything I wrote. Each task is clearly spelt out. This is unique because my handwriting is so bad that Lori usually has to do her best to decipher what the task actually is. If she hadn't been working for me for three plus years, she would probably ask on most every Post-It. My handwriting is not all that bad, but I do not take the extra second, and I do mean second, to write legibly.

With space pretty well cleared on my desk, I sit back and look down at all the papers with the Post-Its. Lori is going to expect me to write like this from here on out. Now I am afraid. I'm smiling, yet at the same time feeling overwhelmed at the thought of having to take an extra second on another day. Today okay, but I am not going to waste the rest of my life. Wow, quite a small battle going on in my head, all because I took a few extra seconds.

I get up and walk over to Lori's desk to place the papers on the corner. I usually spread everything all over her desk so that she can see the things that she needs to do. And what does she usually do with them? Pick them all up and put them in a stack on the corner of her desk.

"I'm learning some pretty unique things about Jim so far today," comes out my mouth suddenly. I feel like a schoolboy who has just learned a basic math problem, so darn proud and wanting to share. It's probably basic to the majority of the world's population, but to me, right here, right now, I have just climbed Mount Everest, so please don't burst my bubble and tell me I only took the first 10 steps up.

"Oh, and what is that, Mr. Goddard?" she inquires, as she turns from her computer and gives me direct eye contact.

"Lori, this is wild. I have learned so many small things today that are really no big deal, but are a big deal." I stop talking for a second and reflect because I want to phrase this in the best Secret format I possibly can instead of staying focused on the negative behavior (not necessarily negative behavior, but hiccups in my traits). I then slowly start again, and say, "By slowing down and taking time to do and enjoy what is in my life, I am seeing things in such a better and different light."

"Take the Post-Its there, Lori, check out my handwriting," a proud look on my face. "You can read it, and all I did was slow down, relax and stay in the moment. Usually, I would be already doing emails in my head while writing the notes, and while on emails, I would be on my phone calls." I lean my bum against the desk that I was on before and shake my head. "And I was just thinking how I go on my emails, and out of the 20 or so messages that will be there, I focus on one and get all bummed out because it has a slightly negative tone to it. Imagine that I can have two people email me about wanting to sell their homes, the opportunity of tens of thousands of dollars, and I stay focused on the Center Road lady because she was drinking too much at 10 last night and sent me a nasty email?" Shaking my head, I carry on, "And I know the only reason she is that way is because she has a lot of stress in her life. Yet I decide that email is important and have it be my focus instead of the wonderful things that are out there."

I get up and walk closer to Lori, "Normally I would dwell upon that for the next few hours and think of how sick I am of real estate. Why? Why would I do that to myself?"

"I think it is hard not to have that stuff affect you," she starts to say when I hold up my hand.

"This is that one day, Lori, that I need you. Hold in there with me. I need you. It is wrong for me to let that have as much power as I have given it in the past. It is a choice I have been making, whether I want to admit it or not. I can also choose to focus on all the good emails and make them important instead, but in the past, I have not. Today is different, and I am glad; it feels better this way. Do you know what I mean? It is tough to fight oneself, but it's a healthy fight."

"Yes, I understand," she says and opens her mouth to say something but does not. She just smiles. I feel she was about to give value to the negative again and caught herself.

"Tomorrow we will talk about this, Lori. Today we are experimental lab animals." Shaking my head, "You know, I just couldn't get myself to say rats. I don't really like them... So we will just consider ourselves human animals today," I say as I head back to my desk.

My bum wasn't even fully in my chair before Raleane called up to me, "Jim, line 1, please." The first call of the day is about to be had. I start to think, "Oh no, I still haven't gotten my voicemails. I wonder if...." However, I am able to stop it right away. I smile. Whoever it is, I am glad they are calling. I reach out and grab the receiver: "This is Jim. How may I help you?"

How do you like that for an opening? Not bad, huh? It is actually my usual one, or I respond with, "This is Jim," and let it roll from there.

The call is a task-oriented one, a task another should have

done and would be easier for the other party to do; however I am known for being very efficient, partly because of my very efficient assistant Lori. I have a choice to make here: I can let it bother me that another is not doing this or...

I am so up today, I know what my answer will be, and I know the caller feels the smile in my voice. I give them my best, "It would be my pleasure," and end the call.

It would be my pleasure. How do you like that? You know I am going to do it anyway so why not do it with a smile? I lean back so I can see Lori. "Um, Lori, can you do me a favor?" I say and I see her shaking her head in acknowledgement the task is about to be handed off to her.

"Oh you mean the "it would be your pleasure" was code for "okay I will have Lori do it?" She grins because this is not the first time we have had this exchange, and I decide to take another step.

"Lori, you're a great worker, person and friend. I am so glad we work together." My eyes widen for further emphasis, "I really am," and then I explain the task.

Perhaps I should get my voicemails, and I reach forward. I notice that I hit the button with a little more energy in my hand than usual. 9:28 and I feel on top of the world. I feel like I have done a day's work already and I haven't even started. It is because the work is different that I feel like I have achieved so much because it has not been the same old same old today. I feel I have learned and grown.

"You have eight new voice messages," and I think, "Oh, rats, I should have…" Nope. Secret, Jim, Secret. I sit up taller than I usually do (I am a sloucher) and think that there is going to be some good stuff here and I am glad these people have made contact. First voice message: I start to write on my oversized daily pad. Off to the second and third, until done, and then I get ready to change my greeting. Oh, we are going to do a humdinger here today. I press 3, then 2, then 2, and show time. In my best voice, "It's Friday, and what a beautiful day it is! The sun is shining and how can you not be excited to be a part of life. Please do leave me a message and I will get back to you as soon as possible. Thank you very much for calling."

Ahh…. I hang up and smile to myself once again. Now that will knock someone's socks off; that will catch them by surprise. Just as I am about to click on my emails, I stop myself. This is just what I was talking about. Off to the next thing while I should have my focus and attention on the tasks at hand. Like I would say to my daughter Marissa, "Focus, Marissa, focus." Perhaps I should take a small dose of my own medicine. I will complete and the return calls or tasks associated and then get my emails.

Fifteen minutes later, I am clicking on Outlook Express and waiting for the messages to arrive. I look down at the lower right hand side, and it says downloading 22 messages. Cool, I say to myself. There will certainly be some good stuff there; I just hope I don't get a bunch of calls. I feel like I need to get these done.

Oh no, did I just give myself the Power of Attraction Kiss

Of Death? Okay, not a Kiss of Death, but the Kiss of Phone Calls? As I lean forward and grab the mouse, I decide that I will do the ones that went into my junk email first. I stop myself. Why would I go to junk first? My answer is that I want to get them out of the way. Wow, why would I want to deprive myself of the good stuff? Sorry junk emails, it is not your time. I thought I was just being efficient, but what I was really doing is keeping myself away from gold.

I move the mouse around and click on the first one when the speaker blares, "Jim, line 2, please, Jim, line 2." Hmm…. I wonder how many of these I cursed, I mean blessed, myself with.

"This is Jim. How may I help you?" I answer. After a hesitation, the caller gets round two: "Elaine! I am glad you called. No, please, don't feel you are bothering me, I consider it a joy every time I hear your voice."

Elaine's house is under agreement, and she is older and only has herself, so she gets worried. She feels she is being a pest, when I actually wish she were my own Grandmother.

After talking for a little bit and reassuring her, I hang up and lean back with reflection. I treat her differently. I really like her. She really likes me…. I think I should treat every client and customer just like her. My clients would be so much nicer and different. My relationships with them are business. I make short phone calls, short emails, short visits; if you ask anyone, they will tell you I am a good businessman.

I take out a small notepad. It is one of Lisa's old ones:

Everything Lisa Lists Turns To Sold. Ahhh…. we thought we were geniuses when we came up with our slogans. Me, the Marketing Maniac, and her with Everything Lisa Lists Turns To Sold.

I scratch out on the pad: Why am I so short on all my calls? Why all business? Then I set it to the side and reach for the mouse again.

This time, I am able to pound through the emails and I am so glad for all the good stuff that was there; I even went out of my way not to just be to the point on the replies. I tried to add a "Have a great day," or "Make this your best day ever," or even "How is the family?" Very uncomfortable actually, but at the same time, it felt good. I have to make sure my mind decides that the recipient will smile and feel good when they see the email. This is not the normal Jim, I am sure some will be thinking. Wow, what's with Jim today? Hey, honey, get this. Seems like Jim is off his rocker a little today!

I lean back after making some return calls and putting some more tasks on Lori and reflect. I would normally dive head first into my prospecting time to find more buyers and sellers. Yet I feel like I need a tune-up first, and I get up and walk into Lisa's old office. Before I close the door, I turn and ask Lori to please take my calls for about 15 minutes, which like everything else, she very happily does. Even in this writing I really wonder if I truly tell her enough how great an employee and person she is?

I close the door and open my hand. In it is the infamous piece of paper with my questions on it. Why am I so focused on just business? I head over to sit on the floor to meditate for a few minutes to gather my thoughts and refocus.

QUIET THE NOISE
AND CENTER ON
WHAT IS IMPORTANT

CHAPTER 8 - MEDITATING

I sit as comfortably as I can. I look up and see the clock. 10:33. I feel good; I have gotten so much done and have done it in a relaxed fashion. I take a deep breath in and close my eyes, trying to regulate my breathing. A true meditator I am not; however, I have learned to hear the loud noise in my head and focus on that. It is like a whistling noise and I can get it to be so loud.

In out, in out, slow, deep, easy. I feel my mind going blank and then I feel thoughts coming from every direction and I try to keep them at bay. After a few minutes, I focus on my question. Why am I all business?

I know the answer, but do not want to put the value to it. In my upbringing, the most important thing in life was work. No questions asked. We never tried to figure out what number 2, 3 or 4 was; we just knew what number 1 was. Now at 45, I have come to the realization that this is not proper. I have done a great job spending wonderful time with my family, yet there are areas I still need to work on. I rush through each and every day and have not put enough importance on people.

Deep breath in, slow out, feeling the beauty of the air. So

clean, so nice, one of those things that you take for granted. Ahhhh.

Being all business is not one of my beliefs any longer. I have decided that, yet, if I want to remove that belief, I need to replace it with a different one. I must reword this and make it an affirmation. It feels so good now that I take the extra moment and give time to all those I come in contact with. Yeah, that will be my new one, as I smile to myself. Yet still at this moment, I feel a bit uncomfortable with this. It simply means I need to grow more here. I know that, but I have already learned today how good it feels and how little time is involved in getting so much in return.

Jim, you are so relaxed and spend wonderful one-on-one time with the clients and customers you work with. You do such a great job taking that small amount of extra time, because time is plentiful. Yeah, that's the ticket.

I breathe in again and wonder if I have other limiting beliefs that I imposed on myself? I do not need any more of them and I think that I should try to study myself further. I truly believe if I do, a higher quality of life will come from it.

With my eyes open, a huge, simple thought comes into my head. Just as I allowed my father to impose his values upon me, I must be careful what I impose upon my own children. My eyes go wide. *Or* those I come in contact with day in and day out. Nodding my head, I realize the importance of being nice and saying nice things all the time. There is such high value to it. I am not going to try to figure out why, but we as human animals are not as kind as we should be. We "joke," which is a label we throw on cutting other people down far too often.

45. I am so glad I am only 45. I have 30 years of going out to the world and saying and doing nice things. It always feels good when you hear or see the nice stuff. We love to watch the movie where that is the main theme, and go awww that was beautiful. We may even share that theme with other people for a day or so after, and then we let it fade and we fall back into life.

Life, the label we keep throwing on it. What is really happening is that we decide to put higher value to all the yuk around us. We focus far too much of our energy on that and make that important. We then share that with those we come in contact with. What if I start a conversation with others with, "Hey, tell me something good," and got the juices flowing toward positive energy right away? Or if they are to venture down the road of misery, ask them that question then or point out to them something nice. I know, I will say something nice to them like, "That shirt looks nice on you. Where did you get it?"

I look up at the clock. It has only been 14 minutes, but it feels like it has been hours of contemplation in a nice relaxed manner. I feel good. I like doing this. It was something I fought. Meditating, it sounded silly. Me sit still? It is what lazy people do. How can you accomplish anything while sitting still? "Get up, you lazy son-of-a-gun and do something." That is what I would think or say. Plus, if you talked to me about meditating, I would say, "Hello, A.D.H.D. here; you're barking up the wrong tree." Yet in reading *The Secret*, it was a common thread for all the different people who contributed.

Rhonda, I really applaud you for being able to gather such a wide range of people that understand that whatever you believe, you can achieve. By reading the book and studying the people on the street, at my work or any place, it is so easy to see this. The tough part was (ahh.... notice I say was) being able to see and believe it in yourself. Think about it; it's so easy to see the traits in others, but if asked about our own, we, just as anyone else would, subconsciously support our current beliefs.

Getting up, I wait for the blood to run back into my legs properly and take a few slow steps into the other office. I feel real good inside and want to think about more things, yet at the same time, I feel I have achieved both so little and so much. The so little are the tiny thoughts that seem so life changing. When meditating, I see, feel, and understand the power of so many things and how easy it is to bring about whatever it is you want. I need to create needs. I need to convince myself that I need to take the time each and every day to meditate, just as I take time each day to eat or brush my teeth or go to the bathroom. I know that if I take a small amount of time every day, the quality of my life and all that I want to achieve can be done so much easier and more joyfully. If I simply take the time.

So if the last statement above is true, why do we not? I must be careful here. It is not that all do not; it is that *most* of the human animals do not. However, there are certain human animals that do and they are the ones we read about, that have this high, wonderful, clear quality of life. And if I was suddenly to decide I want to be an average human being and come up with "reasons" why meditating is not all that it is cracked up to be, I could do that easily. I can then carry on with my life as I was. No harm, no foul. It is a simple choice for me to make. However if I am to make that choice, I must not scorn those who do meditate; I must be happy with my choice and decision and be happy for those who have made another choice.

In thinking this, I also come up with another thought. I used to think happy people were fake. Just because I was not raised in a warm, loving family does not mean there are not warm, loving families out there. Some people allow themselves to truly feel love in the presence of someone else and others. Wow, I suddenly think, how cool would that be? To allow yourself to love fully, deeply in the moment, and not destroy the present moment with thoughts of the hurt past or fear of the future. Imagine loving and being with someone special and staying right in the moment. There are those that are real; they are not fake, I am thinking. I want that, I proclaim suddenly, and as I think about this, I realize I am with someone who also wants that.

Sitting back in my chair, I still find myself contemplating all that has been going on today. My day has definitely gone better than any other day in a long time, and usually how my day goes correlates with a listing or a sale. I realize that I have achieved so little today, and yet so much. I feel great and want to feel this more and more.

I look over at the phone. Okay, today I will touch people

with nice things. I will ask about the kids, family, or whatever comes to my mind. I will not be all business today. Being all business is not the most important thing. Then I look over and realize I have more emails.

Okay, power of attraction, I am going to get some great business stuff now. I had wanted the business stuff to chill so I could achieve all this other stuff that I decided was important today, so do your thing. I lean forward and grab the mouse with a confused smile on my face. The confusion is the clearness of seeing things right this minute. This is nothing new, but all this time, others who are important to me have told me these things, but I did not listen. Success was the most important thing; if you want to succeed, you need to work harder and smarter than all the others. That is what I have done. You don't achieve the sales I have had by not working harder and smarter. That is where the mistake is. That was my belief, and I do not want to believe that anymore. I look forward to talking to Lisa about this at lunch. Actually, I think I probably could have achieved so much more while working so much less if I had realized before. All I would have had to do is change my belief structure. As the thought flies through my head, I feel as if I should write that sentence down and read it again and again until I understand the truth to it and believe it in terms of how true it actually is.

WHAT BELIEFS DO YOU WANT TO CHANGE?

1)

2)

3)

4)

5)

YOUR LIFE TODAY
IS WHAT YOU <u>BELIEVE</u>
IT SHOULD BE

CHAPTER 9 - WHATEVER YOU BELIEVE YOU WILL ACHIEVE

I let go of the mouse and focus for a second. If I need to change my belief structure, now is as good a time as any. Let's consider this a game. If this stuff was to really work, you know the Power of Attraction (which I have seen, felt, and lived so far today), and whatever you believe, you will achieve, how would I play this game? Let's just say for a minute here that it actually works. What would the steps be?

Want. Yes, that's right. I need to identify what I want. What do I want? What do I want? That should be easy. My eyes go to the left and up, thinking, what do I want? Nice car, have it. Beautiful wife, yup. Big warm comfortable house, check. I know: money money, money. But how much is the question. I want more and right now that seems kind of like a sickness. Think about it. I have more than 95% of the population, but I will work long and hard hours for what? So I can wish I spent more time with the wife and kids.

I always thought it was kind of insane when I knew my father was working hard to create a better life for us all (even though at a younger age I felt it was only for himself), yet the only thing we really ever did together was work. I spent time with Mom and Dad, working. I felt like his slave, not his son. Although I am sure he would be able to come up with some fun things we did. Ahhh, I catch myself suddenly. I did do things with him. He took me to the Red Sox game with Mr. Lapointe, and he took me and a friend to Canobie Lake Park one year. He also went to…. I stop here. I get the point of my human lab rat James Goddard. I can come up with more, but for some strange reason, I had focused on the other things. Here it is, I feel like I am so smart and have it so together when I have so much room left for growth. I guess the most important part is to allow the growth.

So what do I want? This easy question just became so much harder. If I really, really had a choice, what would I want? I feel stuck. I should have a thousand things rushing at me, and right this minute, I cannot come up with any.

Alright, I am going to be logical here. I want more listings and sales, and I want to be able to get them in a healthy manner, not all at once. This will give me more money and have me be more relaxed and make it so I will spend more time with the wife and kids. Yeah, that's the ticket. But wait, I also want to work less and still achieve this.

There are certainly more steps than this involved, so what would be the next step? I lean back again and am focused on the upper left of my eyes, not sure what I am trying to see there, but my eyes and face sure are focused on that area. Visualize. I need to visualize this. I would imagine that I would have to visualize this in many ways. Like seeing all the listings I have or seeing myself going out to appointment after appointment or seeing the phone light lit up or the emails pouring in asking me to list the property.

I look over to the right and am imagining my files there being full of pending sales. Not just a few, but so many that are waiting to close. I see myself doing an online search and me being the top agent in closed transactions out of the approximately 600 Coldwell Banker Residential Brokerage agents in NH. Okay, I need to make sure I visualize this in many, many ways, and keep doing that.

Acting, not like the people in Hollywood, but then again, maybe. If I am going to have all that is above, I need to act in this way. I need to act like I have all these listings and sales, not just here in my office, but at all times. In the general public, at home, on appointments. I need to have the confidence of the person that would have all these things already.

What's next? If I am going to play this game (I need to make sure I do not convince myself that this is just a game; I need to convince myself this is all real and all going to happen), I need to believe in order to achieve. If I truly reflect on where exactly I am here today, I do have to say I believed I could achieve all this; that is why I have it all. Now why can't I just change my belief patterns a little bit and achieve at a higher level?

I can, that's just it. I can! That is what all these people who have broken through are telling us. You can break through and you can achieve whatever you want if you believe. They are trying to tell us they are not "just lucky" that they believed and made changes in their lives because they believed. So you and I can, too. Kind of funny, we know that if we dedicate ourselves in certain ways, we can achieve anything. If I wanted to bulk up and have more muscle, can we agree that if I took a 30 to 45 day period, ate right, and worked out for 30-45 minutes a day, I would be in much better shape at the end of that time? It is a no-brainer. Perhaps this mind stuff, that if you believe, you can achieve is Simple Simon. It really is that easy. It certainly sounds like that is what they are trying to tell us.

Alright, if I am as smart as I think I am, I can do this! What else? I declared my want, visualized it, and need to act that way. Maybe I should get some visuals and put them in a prominent place for myself to see all the time. A constant reminder that will show me what I am going to achieve. They say that will help me to believe more fully and deeply. A visualization board, I can do that; it's just a matter of when. Usually I would say I am just too darn busy. It is a good idea, but I just don't have the time to fit that in. However, today we are approaching things a little differently.

I pull out my pen, lean forward, and find my daily schedule. I figure I need about an hour to do this. I also know that if I write this down, it increases the probability of me doing it. It makes me think of a study that was done in which the success of a group with a written business plan was measured against a group without a business plan. The success of the students that did have the written business plan was just overwhelming. This always had me trying to get my agents to write out their business plans, and I was amazed how they just wouldn't do it. No matter how hard I tried, they had excuses or things that they allowed to stop themselves from writing it out. Boy, this sure does tie in real well with *The Secret*; they really did not believe, they could not see themselves succeeding or at least taking it to a higher level. Well, that's not going to be me. If it can be done, I am going to do this.

2:00 to 3:00 today, I write in my schedule, and suddenly another example comes into my head. For example, the drunk down on the streets of Boston, it is his goal to get a drink today and just like every other day, he will achieve it. He believes, he achieves. That is how it is each day. I need to come up with another more positive example. Then it is hitting me again. They make movies about those who make the breakthrough or have them go on a speaking circuit. They speak on their changes, and people ooh and ahhh as they listen and look forward to trying to make changes in their own lives, but for some reason they do not make the breakthrough. So few can. Why? Why? Why? I want to know why some are able to. Is it really the basic simple success formula that is written in *The Secret*? They write that it has been this way all through time, and I do believe this and I do not feel any of them are or were any smarter than I am. Yet in some way, shape, or form, they were able to rise above, and so many after such insurmountable odds. I want that!

I feel determined and think I am going to put as much effort into this as possible. 2:00 to 3:00, and in the meantime, I am going to will more buyers and sellers, and I am going to start it right now.

Looking down at my files, I think okay, who am I going to call first? Which one of these people needs to sell now, and my direct line rings. "Hello, this is Jim. How may I help you?" I answer with a smile in my voice although I don't know the number.

"Hi, is this James Goddard?"

"You got him."

"Oh, hi this is Mrs. Smith, and I was thinking of selling my home. I was told I should call you."

I'm doing my best not to be freaked out; I get these calls all the time, but it is the timing that has me back pedaling. "Ok, well what I need to do is go through your home for 5 to 10 minutes at some point and see it head to toe. I then will come back, do a computerized analysis, sit with you, and let you know what you can get for your home in today's marketplace. What is a good time to see the home? What works for you?"

I get the appointment booked, and wonder if déjà vu is real or is that just a label that someone threw on the universe bringing you what you are after?

This was just too perfect. I go to my email again. I have six more messages that have come through, and on one, the subject line is an MLS number, so I know it is most likely an inquiry from a buyer.

With a click, I open it and inside I feel differently about this. Usually I think, okay, let's do it, and I work it, but this time I feel it is a buyer that wants to buy this property and will! Oh yeah, it is on one of the ones that I just listed and it is such a good buy. I want to get this appointment. I reach forward and grab the phone, and over the next 3 minutes, I get the appointment. I feel the excitement in my voice, so much so that even my assistant Lori wants to see the place and she already has.

I hang up, and look over at Lori. She is smiling at me. "Nice job, Mr. Goddard," she says and is shaking her head a little. "You were really going for it; you're going to sell that, I just know it."

"Oh, you just know it. Why do you say that?" I respond, with a quizzical look on my face, but I kind of know what the answer is already. She was feeling it. It is the way I made it feel, and she felt it.

"I don't know. You just made it sound so good. It sounded like of course they will buy it, and it is a nice place."

I am nodding my head. That was the energy I had put into it. That was the way I was presenting it to the universe and she felt that and didn't really even know it. I need to make sure I put that kind of energy and effort into everything. If I do, I could get so much more out of everything. Imagine if I were focused on the positives of every property I came into contact with. Each property was someone's dream at some point, and if it was one's dream, it stands to reason that it could be another's. So many agents focus and see the imperfections and out of their own fears, they scare away what could be the perfect buyer for the home. Without realizing it, they make the buyer feel like an idiot for loving the place. They hear all that is wrong with it from the agent. Sure, they said some nice things, but it sure feels like it would be wrong for us to buy that home.

Whatever I believe, I will achieve, I say to myself and think of others that believe. Tiger Woods believes; he just won that US Open again by getting a birdie to tie Rocco on the 18th hole. He forced the playoff the next day, and the next day, he did the same exact thing on the 18th hole before he won it on the first sudden death playoff hole. He believed, surgically repaired knee and all.

For the next 40 minutes, I do all my catch-up work (which means I gave a bunch of tasks to Lori) and get ready to go meet Lisa for lunch at 12. She had called me to let me know that she could meet then. I have an extra 10 minutes before I have to leave and decide to do this a little differently. Usually, I hop up at the very last second and everyone hears me pound down the stairs as fast as can. It is considered the joke of the office. I quickly check my mailbox, avoid any real conversation, and sign out, saying as I run out the door, "Oh man, I am late again."

Now, please understand, I am not really late. I get to an appointment at exactly the right time or within 2 or 3 minutes. If I get to an appointment 5 to 10 minutes early, I do not know what to do with myself. Today though, I am going to leave early. I am constantly asked questions by the other agents and I half listen, or they go, "Oh. Never mind, I will catch you later." Or I yell back to them that I will call them from the car in two minutes.

I look around the office to make sure I am not forgetting anything (this is another famous thing I do; oh I mean that I used to do). Many times, it takes me two or three tries to leave. I get down the stairs or to my car and realize that I was so focused on being late that I have forgotten my paperwork or grabbed wrong paperwork or have no pen, you name it. I scan the office and put on my suit coat in a very relaxed manner. I let Lori know I will see her in about an hour, and I would love to go over the files with her then and play a little catch up.

I know in her mind she is thinking, yeah right. I follow through about one out of every five times I say that. I end up checking my email and messages again and then most likely I have other tasks that I decide are far more important than playing catch up with her. It is a good thing she is very capable of working on her own. "Good, I have plenty I need to go over," she says smiling and I see a twinkle of doubt as well as a glint of hope too.

Walking down the stairs, I open the door. I see the bathroom door and decide I should go. This is another huge thing; I usually go about 45 minutes after I realize I have to go because it takes time away from tasks and prospecting.

I had an extra 10 minutes, and I still have 8 more to go. I am hopeful of getting to the restaurant a few minutes early, actually, I believe I will, and I head downstairs the rest of the way.

"Hey George, how are you man?" I ask as he looks up from the computer and extends his hand.

"Good, how you doing, Gumby?" (the old college nickname) he responds, as he looks me in the eye and stretches, obviously wishing he had gotten a few extra hours of sleep or one less "dirty" martini last night.

Now I really hop out of character again and sit in the chair next to him. I decide I am going to throw him a compliment and show him I care. I am thinking this is going to be easy but I find myself struggling to come up with something. I am not used to this; I need to make it second nature somehow.

"You sure did great golfing yesterday. Your game is really coming along nicely." I smile to myself, happy I have pulled out a happiness card and shared it. I see George lighting up, but putting on a no-big-deal face at the same time.

"Yeah, my drive is coming nice. Even out-hit you a few times, Gumbo, but I still need to…" This is where I cut him off. This is what we as humans do; he was about to share negative. No, not huge, oh man, he is such a negative type of person data. However, we are in good feelings so we shift to something imperfect to center us perhaps. For some reason right now, it does not make sense to me, yet I do the same thing. I think I will cut out this very unnecessary step.

"Only see the good stuff, George, and build upon it. Do not let the yucky stuff exist and grow. When you see the game in your mind, only visualize those beautiful shots and more of those will come your way. That is the law of the universe."

Getting up, I am looking at him as he starts to speak again, "Yeah, but…" I stop him again, knowing that the Ego is trying to support the behavior. Oh my, Eckhart does say how that is the biggest obstacle to growth, the darn Ego and it trying to defend its decisions. I am just realizing that there is a tie between what Haanel was saying about how the subconscious supports the conscious no matter what, and what Mr. Eckhart is saying about the Ego. I need to think on that one more at some point.

Smiling, I say it again, "Only see the good stuff and that is what will find its way into your life. How's Helen?" Ha! Snuck in a caring question. I stand there walking slowly backwards waiting for a response.

"Good, she's out in California for the week. I have the kids," he says and puts his head back to the computer.

"Okay, man, have a great day. Hope to see you later on," I respond as I am walking toward the back door, thinking to myself, I was golfing with him yesterday and I never knew that. I wonder if he told me and I was just not listening or if since I never ask these things. I just don't know. He's my pal. Why would I not know? Smiling, I realize why the one too many dirties last night; Helen's gone.

LAUGHING AT YOURSELF
HELPS YOU TO GROW

CHAPTER 10 - LUNCH TIME

Driving away from the office and getting on the road is far more relaxing than usual, but I do not really realize it yet. The trip is less than 5 minutes, so it is kind of funny if you think about it. How do I come up with a lame excuse for being late EACH time?

I am so serious here. This is the woman I love, the one who means the most to me, the one I cannot wait to see at night. Remember how I said I am always exactly on time or a minute or two late? Well, I meant for appointments. Not for her, she is different. I am pretty much at best on time, and late 90+ percent of the time, and I do not mean by a minute or two. So what message do you think I am sending to her?

It's quite obvious, really. She does not mean as much to me as pretty much all the other people on the earth. Oh sure, I can have illogical words come flying out my mouth in support of my behavior, but if I was to truly study this human animal today, I would have to say he is sending the wrong message and his behavior is supportive of not caring as much for his wife as he does for all the others.

You know thinking about that doesn't feel good. Oh no,

I feel a restatement coming on here. I am so glad I am now aware of this behavior; it makes it so easy to correct, and my relationship will get better and better now because of this knowledge.

Sitting at the second stop light, I feel my whole face glowing. I am not just smiling; I am glowing. It is the thought of having my relationship with Lisa get even better. If you tried to tell me it could get better and better, I would have smiled and shared with you how wonderful it is already, and what a great life we have etc., etc., etc. My mind would have said, sorry, closed for the day. Perhaps if you come back during a period of pain, I may listen, but the boat is not rocking, so there is no need to put any additional energy or effort into this, but really, thanks for stopping by.

Yes, I do believe that would have answered it fully and correctly. I'm thinking about even this one small issue of being late most all the time with her, the subconscious message that is being handed to her each time, and how I can make a very small change that will increase the connection we have at the core, the subconscious level. Now that is a cool thought, and I wonder how many other things I can come up with.

To heck with this, dude, I made you coffee this morning. See, I love you, or… Alright, I do not want my mind to go to the things I would support. I understand it is normal and natural for my Ego to support my current behavior. Or as *The Master Key* says, my subconscious supports my conscious; it does not question it, it supports it.

I know another one I am going to change as soon as I

see her, I say to myself as I pull into the restaurant, nodding my head as I pull in and not even realizing it. Nodding for so many reasons, acknowledging my behavior and knowing on the inside that what I am going to do is the correct thing for her and me and the reasons I have not are built in belief systems from which I need to detach myself.

As I pull in, I am looking for a space to park, but it is very difficult not to see this lady sitting on the granite bench out in front of the restaurant, with her face lifted slightly in the air to get as much sun as possible, and you can tell she is feeling the rays. Yes, my Lisa in the same place she is almost every time. The only thing that would stop her from being out there is rain.

Getting out, I am looking forward to my change. I walk over to the entryway of the restaurant, I step up on the patio, and she gets up and slightly turns toward the doors. I reach out and touch her right shoulder with my left hand, gently, stopping her. She turns with a slight look of confusion, as if she is supposed to see something that I want to show her. Her quizzical look meets my smiling eyes all of a sudden, and I lower both my arms and spread them to my sides showing her I want a hug.

Her eyes get bigger and light up. The funny thing is I know she has lived for this. She feels love inside and loves to demonstrate that, but I was raised differently: you do not show public forms of affection. You just know I love you, because you know it.

She steps forward into my arms and melts into my chest;

she has waited through nine years of us being together for this. Something so simple that I had not done. I give her hugs at home, out of the public eye, but not out in areas of other human beings. Now there is something to meditate on sometime, huh, Jim? I think as we turn to go in.

Holding the door open for her, I look straight into her eyes and I am having such a hard time not blurting out much too loudly, "Lisa, I have so many things to share with you, it's incredible" (I want to say pathetic, but am able to catch myself on time with this one). "But first how has your morning been?"

"Wait," I say quickly, "Before you tell me that, because I do want to hear about it, I have to tell you. Every time I drive up and see you out front sitting on that bench, you look like a goddess, which is so fitting for this Greek Restaurant, huh?" smiling and seeing her melting at the compliment.

Her head suddenly seems like a turtle's as it bobs forward and the simple words come out of her mouth, "Thank you."

I see the lady at the podium, looking at us. She has a really big, from-the-heart smile on today, and I feel as if she is feeding off the energy Lisa and I are giving off right now. We have created our environment like we always do, but are slightly more aware of it today than usual. There is happiness around us, and that is what we see and feel right now. Good luck to someone or something trying to change it.

She opens her mouth to speak. It was a much longer silence than usual; she was slightly mesmerized by the universe that was in front of her and liking it. Nevertheless, before she can speak, I smile and say, "Two, please."

She is already holding two menus in her hands, holding them against her heart, and she turns and asks us to follow her with her body language, knowing nothing verbal is needed with us. I step back so Lisa can go first, and we venture to a special spot. How do I know it is special? Because everything is special in my world today. I had decided this morning that it would be, no matter what, remember.

Sitting down, I want to stretch out my neck and start to tell her all the things that have been in my day, but I ask, "Now, please tell me about your morning."

As she goes over all the different things she has done, I ask a few probing questions here and there so she knows I am interested, that what she does is important to me. Usually, in my mind I can't wait to tell her something that is special in my life, and we skip over her to hear mine. Today it is so nice having her share with me.

A small time later, she sits back a little; she was really stretched forward telling me all her stuff about her website and the affiliate program. As her back hits the seat, she chimes in, "So, please tell me, what is it that you are so excited to share?"

"I am not sure which thing I want to share first," I say as I lean forward and project my voice right at her. "Both things I want to share are such small things, but yet so big. Do you remember when you asked me before when was I going to realize I do not have to work longer, harder hours in order to make more money? That if I really believed in *The Secret,* I shouldn't have to." Shaking my head slightly side to side as I say this, "I don't know why I was not listening to you more on that. I guess I knew you were right, but at the same time, I was so focused on wanting to make more money that I didn't want to take a chance. Plus, that goes against traditional modern day, every day person kind of mentality."

"I finally realized it this morning. I don't have to work harder and longer, so why am I? Especially when there are so many other things in life that are far more important?"

I lean back now and have a slightly exasperated look on my face, "I don't know why I decided I needed to work longer and harder. I mean we both know business has been great this year for me. The market is down almost 25% in the area, yet things are going great, and I don't have to work longer to do what I am or to achieve even more."

Now she is the one smiling. "Well, it is about time you realized that, because you have been the *Secret* person, and yet you would not apply it to that part of your life for some reason," she says almost sternly, but holding back a bona fide I-told-you-so.

"So what else did you want to share?" she asks, figuring that maybe she can grab another small victory and keep this going while I am allowing myself to be dissected.

"You're really going to laugh at this one, honey. Driving to work today and driving here, I didn't get behind anybody slow, and the reason I did not get behind anyone slow was I was relaxed and was just taking my time rather than rushing to get to where I am going as fast as I can."

"Usually, I leave at the very last second. I know that and have to admit it. Because of that, I can't have any slowness factor in there or I am screwed, so that is why I am always complaining about the people in front of me."

From the look on her face, I know she wants to say, "Duh, Jim," but for some strange reason, this is a hiccup in my own behavior that I feel is huge to have noticed. I shake my head and I'm smiling big. "You want to say no kidding, huh?"

"Jim, I have told you for years. When you all of a sudden decide it is time to go, it is time to go. You expect us to pick up and go that second."

I pull my lips back across my teeth and remind myself, only for a day, Jim. I have the slight feelings of wanting to defend that it isn't always like that, but if I am being real, it sure is the majority of the time. I take a deep breath in and say it firmly, "I know."

I feel I must have the look on my face of the kid who just had to admit to something he didn't want to, because I am seeing her eyes start to get a little squinty as she starts to smile, and she looks like she adores me, and says, "I love you so much."

My sheepish smile creeps in and my head goes down a little. I say nicely, "Thank you, honey, I love you, too."

The rest of the meal was really uneventful, yet very enjoyable. Lisa did ask me if I would go to Jamie's softball game today, and the typical answer would be either, "I can't" or "We'll see," which is just a delayed no. I gave it thought and instead said I would try my best and give her a call later on.

After I pay and as we are going out, I am trying to remember if I would normally kiss her goodbye or not. I really cannot remember if I would. It would be like me not to do that in public. It isn't right, is what my upbringing instilled in me. Either way, I feel my more normal departure would be to tell her I love her, thanks for coming to lunch, and see you tonight. Then it hits me, yes, sometimes I do kiss her, but only if she is in her car and people are not looking. Then I can lean in and give her a little peck on the lips.

Not today, my friends. I stand out front after she comes through the door I was holding for her, and I stretch out my arms again smiling. Not only do I give her a hug, I give her a kiss. Am I an animal or what?

WHO ARE YOU GOING TO TELL YOU LOVE THEM?

1)

2)

3)

4)

5)

REMOVE THOSE SHACKLES
YOU HAVE KEPT SO FIRMLY
IN PLACE.

CHAPTER 11 - BACK AT THE OFFICE

Pulling in the driveway of the office, I have the feel and pull of, I don't want to be here today. Yet we all know Jim has to work longer and harder than anyone else or else. Or else! I wonder what wild subconscious supported things I can come up with for that ridiculous thought-process. I am sure I could come up with a plethora of reasons that will sound silly to you, yet real to me, to support that thought.

Walking up the stairs to the third floor, I am going over this in my head. How many times have I thought I would like to go home, but since it is only 4:30, I can't? Mainly because I need to make more calls, emails, money, prospect a little longer; be here in case some buyer or seller calls. It is even hard for me to go home at six or seven. I do have to say, at eight, I don't ever feel like I should be here still.

Going up the last set of steps, I am also thinking on the days that I get in the office before eight. I feel okay. If I am after that, I feel like I am late. Can you imagine that? I feel like I have wasted the first half of the day. Wow, I have a few more hiccups I want to iron out today, and since I am playing this game only for today, I will see to it that I get the most out of it.

Coming around the corner at the top of the stairs and into my office, Lori is sitting there with her back to me and asks, "So, how was lunch Mr. Goddard?"

"Better than you could ever imagine. I am so glad I took the time out of my day and do not know why I don't do that every day! However, I do have a question for you." I lean down in with a smirk-like smile and say, "Are you ready to meet?"

Holy Toledo, I am thinking, as I feel like I just set down a wind up toy. She immediately grabs a few things from a pile and starts asking questions. She is speaking so quickly, I have not actually heard what she really said. She has a what-do-you-think look on her face. "Okay, Lori, you know how I write too fast, and it makes it hard for you to read and you want me to slow down and write so you can actually read it?"

"Yeah," she says smiling and wanting to spout some examples but I am not going to let her.

"Well, I didn't get a single thing you just said, dude." Grinning ear to ear. "Slow down. I swear I will give you 20 minutes. Will that be enough time?"

"I'll take it and see what we can do," she says smiling back at me and talking a little slower. For the next 20 minutes, she asks questions on things where I almost want to say, geez, I don't know, what do you think? But I am the one who is the boss. I am supposed to come up with all the answers and with confidence. We weed through many things that were hanging for her that she needed my guidance on because they were not decisions for her to make just by herself. Yet after we finished I was thinking to myself, all my clients, and yes, I do mean all, are right. I am lucky to have her. I feel like I tell her that but wonder if she would agree.

"Lori," I say just before I sit back down at my desk, "I really appreciate all you do. You're a great worker and person. Do you feel I tell you that, or do you feel I never do?"

"No, you tell me that, but thank you, it does feel good to hear," as she has a smile on her face and turns back to her computer feeling all good inside.

I sit down and think if I am nice to one more person, I am going to go out of my head, joking of course, but why would I joke like that? Really, this has been one of the most wonderful days of my life so far and it is only 1:35. I feel so great inside and I refuse to let other feelings stop these feelings from growing. I can already say I feel better than I thought I could and I bet that I can feel even better. It is just that I do not allow myself to; I pull myself back down to earth or blame it on someone else, when really I have only done it to myself because I needed it and did not realize it. Wow, what a concept that is, huh? My inner self thinking or feeling that I was feeling too good and that it needed to stop. What the hell is that?

Rephrase. I am so glad that I was able to identify that and no longer bring myself down when I am feeling up. I now let myself keep thinking good thoughts and feeling the goodness of life.

Okay, I have not checked my emails or voicemails since 11:45. Usually I would be stressing out because of that, but today I know it is no big deal. Everything is going to work out perfectly no matter what. I push the voicemail button on the phone and wait to hear how many there are.

"You have 6 new messages, and 23 saved messages, main menu to listen." I hit the one to hear the first message before the voicemail lady blurts out my other options and then pound through the messages one after another before I jump to the emails.

After about 25 minutes of tasks, making calls, and emails, I decide I am going to continue to step out of the comfort zone and do one of those things you wish you do, but do not. I am going to visit my parents. You may view this as, oh, that is nice, but it really is not that simple. The relationship has been strained for years. Each time I go and speak with them (my father that is), I am hit with the same old unproductive crap and questions. For the last five plus years at least, I chat for a few minutes, and then end up smiling and saying, "Well I have to go. Have a great day," and then question myself in the car: Why did I put myself through that again?

Today is going to be different though. For some reason, I just know everything is going to work out perfectly. Especially with all the readings I have done; I really feel *The Power of Now* is the one that will help me the most. Eckhart is saying we judge today's events and react to it based upon something that happened in the past. It really is not fair to the current event to do this. Imagine if you were judged on how you were 20 years ago!

I am going to go meet and chat with them and allow whatever I would have viewed as crap in the past to flow right through me.

"Lori, I am calling it a day. If you need me, you can get me on my cell phone; otherwise I will see you tomorrow, buddy," as I have this smile that is taking over my face. I feel like the kid that has successfully gotten a cookie from the cookie jar with no one looking. I am going to take the rest of the day off! I feel naughty, but happy and excited that I am allowing myself to do this.

As I get up, I look down at my schedule and see I have something written in from 2:00 to 3:00. I lean down to see it better. I don't remember an appointment... Then it hits me as I see it: the visualization board. I stand back up straight and tall and am wondering what is most important right now. Part of me wants to get out of here; feeling like I always have a reason not to leave work, but this is not really a work-related item. I could simply write in an hour tomorrow; that would be easy enough, plenty of time available then.

I sit back down and decide to view the other side of the coin. They say how important visualizations are and I do feel I have not put enough value in that. Am I being just like the agents who do not want to write out a business plan? I think even deeper on this.

We all have visuals in our lives. Look around yourself. You have filled your life, walls, tables, pocketbooks, body, you name it, with visuals. These are the things that you believe are important to you and that you have attracted into your life.

If I or anyone truly desires to attract something different into our lives, we need to take some intellectual steps here in order to do such. We have to have some sort of discipline just like those we watch on TV. We cheer them on and want them to do and take steps we wish we could, yet we do not. Well, remember, today is the day that is to be different. I will take off to see my parents *and* get working on the visualization board.

I look over at my other work desk; that is the place to start this. It is about to become my visualization desk. "Lori, I need you," I say suddenly, knowing I want to shorten this to 30 minutes and also do 30 tomorrow.

As I get up and move to the other desk, I turn to her and ask, "Can you please go on the computer and find some pictures of me with the kids and with Lisa?"

Sitting in the chair, I pull out a few highlighters of different colors and grab a piece of cardboard-like paper. I look at it and decide that just isn't good enough, and see a dry erase board I have. Yes, now that's what I am after, nodding my head up and down. Now what are the things I want to bring into my life more? I need to identify them.

Pulling out a piece of paper, I start to write out a few. Wine cellar, oh yeah that's one. Looking up and down all the shelves trying to decide which special bottle you are going to crack open, which great country's bottle or what year.... Mmmm... I am smiling ear to ear on that thought and I dream about it. Well, that is one. A camper, there's another. I so want to take a few months off and drive across country and see all that is out there. There are so many special sites and pleasures that I have wanted to see and experience. I can so imagine looking across at Lisa, seeing her face radiate from all the beauty we are driving by. Yup, there's number two. Now what else do I want to visualize?

Leaning back now, I am wondering what else would be a wonderful vision I want to have and hold and keep in front of me each and every day. Family. My family. I will need to get some pictures from home of the different trips we took, like going up Mount Washington, or Lake George New York, or the Pocono Mountains in Pennsylvania when we stayed there in a resort for a week.

I turn now and have my chair face Lori, "Okay, Lori, you with me for a second here? I need you to go online and get me the best pictures you can of..." and I read her off my list. "And please make sure that you get me colorful, beautiful, wonderful pictures, and that wine cellar picture, please make sure that cellar is full. Once you get those pictures, please put them on my desk here so tomorrow I can label them and get them on my visualization board. Also on the pictures of Lisa and I or the kids, print off a lot of those on scrap paper so I can have choices as to which ones."

I look down at the white board and can imagine the pictures of Lisa, the kids and me in the very center and the other dreams working outward from there. This is going to be fun.

Knowing that I have taken some positive first steps to achieve a wonderful visualization board, I feel I can call it a day.

Down the stairs I go, feeling like I have such a jump in my step, a relaxed jump. As I go by the other agents, I touch them on the shoulder or simply ask how they are doing as I make my way to the sign out board and then out the back door. As I go out, I feel how warm and sunny it is, kind of a funny feeling. I don't usually let myself enjoy this time or part of the day, so it seems so funny and wonderful to be out in this. I am actually looking at the day and every thing in it in such a different manner right now.

In my car I go. I feel I do have the proper mindset for this meeting with Mom and Pop. The drive is smooth and easy once again. I do have to say that my thoughts were going every which way as I drove, feeling and reviewing so many things as I went. It is hard to believe all that I reviewed in my mind during those 14 minutes. As each car I drove by, it would hit me as *The Secret* says: whatever you believe you will achieve. Each person believed that what he or she is driving is what he or she deserved; you can see it in each and every one. Now if that really is that basic a premise, it should be easy to change with simple awareness of this. Awareness of what, though?

I am trying so hard to tie it all together as I drive, *The Power of Attraction* and whatever you believe you will achieve. We attract whatever we believe; it finds its way into our lives.

That is what it is with all out there, we the human animal. So if I change what I believe and take on all the characteristics of what I want, it has no choice but to find its way into my life. That's cool. Now I just have to put some good thought into what it is that I want. Funny that is what I keep coming back to. What do I truly want?

WHAT DO YOU TRULY WANT?

1)

2)

3)

4)

5)

THE ONLY BATTLE YOU HAVE
IS WITH YOURSELF.

CHAPTER 12 - HI DAD

I pull into the store, oh yes, the store. I should probably share a little on that. He has one of the nicest Garden Centers in New Hampshire. He purchased it as a gift shop back in 1970, and here, 38 years later, it is a beautiful place to see, enjoy, and hopefully purchase some of the nicest and widest varieties of plants and shrubs ever.

I park about 10 spaces away from the door. Pop likes to save the closer spaces for customers that are looking to hop in and get out. Wanting to start this off in the most positive fashion possible, I do this small thing and know it will get better and better.

As I get out of the car, I am seeing the actual flowers more than usual. I am smiling big as I look at the pretty faces of the pansies as I make my way to the front door. Looking up, I see an older woman appreciating the flowers also. I slow down to a near stop and smiling at her say, "They're beautiful, aren't they? I just love pansies, don't you?" Knowing full well by the warmth she has in her face that she is a true fan.

"Oh my yes, they have always been a favorite for me. My mother used to have them grow right next to the vegetable garden off the front porch. I would get up first thing in the morning and put my shoes on sitting on the top step and see them." She is looking off at something, seeing the vision from so many years ago. "And when the wind would blow, they would sway back and forth like a group of children wanting to play. I always felt they waited for me each day, and this was their way of saying hello to me."

I had come to a full stop when she started talking, so now I am next to her making direct eye contact so she knows I am here listening and fully understanding what she is feeling and saying, instead of the typical passing by and not acknowledging a fellow human being. Far too much of that in life, but I changed that right here, right now. Reaching out and placing a hand on her soft shoulder, I look directly in her eyes and say, "That sounds like such a great memory. I really appreciate you sharing that with me; it makes my day," and I widen my smile and carry on by making my way to the front door.

The doors are open today. Many sets of doors are to allow the air to flow freely. Around the corner and, "Hey, Ab," to my sister, "Where's ma and pa?"

"Oh, he has gone next to door to rest. He usually only makes it to 11 or 12, and then he is too pooped out. Plus he didn't take his pills as he drove cross country last week so he isn't feeling all that well."

"Oh, so you think it is nicer when he's not over here, do you?" smiling big, knowing that the atmosphere is so much more relaxed when he is non-existent.

"You think, maybe?" she blurts out with her eyebrows raised.

"So, how is every thing with you?" A question that I am not sure I have ever asked her in my life.

"Good, we have so much to do. We're trying to get stuff planted down at the house and keep this place cooking at the same time. It's that time of the year," she says, knowing I full well understand. We were all raised in this and know this business inside and out. However, also notice her answer was 100% about work. Work is the most important thing in life; that is the belief structure that was imposed upon us (or you could say we allowed to be imposed upon us). I did actually ask her how she was, not how is the store, yet that is how I would have answered the same question if she would have asked it of me.

"Have a great day, you guys," I say to the employees as I walk out and head toward my parent's apartment next door. I pretty much know them all but also think right now that I do not really know them. I wonder why?

As I walk, I am doing my gratitudes in my head again. Ahh so thankful for this warm sunny day, this clean fresh air, the beautiful car I drove over in, these wonderful clothes I am wearing, and the fact I have family.

Their apartment is above the convenience store they also own. I come through the door and see Ernie. I like Ernie; he is a guy with simple wants in life and a great attitude. "Hey Ernie, how are you man?" I ask as I come through the door.

"Great, you having all kinds of fun today are you?" a typical Ernie question; he usually starts saying "Merry Christmas" in September.

"This is the greatest day in my life so far, you have no idea," I say smiling and leaving him almost not knowing what to say. "My parents are upstairs, right?" pointing up in the air as I take a step behind the counter. You have to take the stairs behind the counter to get up there and I want to show Ernie the respect of asking instead of just invading his space.

"Yeah, I think so," he says. "I saw your mother go up a little while ago. I haven't seen your Dad at all today."

"Maybe he snuck up the back way," I say as I head up the stairs and open the first door. There are two doors to the apartment. The first one you walk into a storage area for the business, and then come to a second door. I knock a soft knock, knowing I can just walk in, but want to give them the respect and not just barge in like the others do.

Ten seconds later, the door opens and there is Mom leaned over a little, peering out the door with a bowl in her hand. She gives her normal response, "Oh, hello there. I thought I heard a knock. Come in. How have you been?" she asks as she turns to go into the living room, bringing me to the bedroom where Dad is surely on the computer placing bets on races all over the United States.

"Things are great, Mom, thanks for asking. How does it feel to be back?" They will be here for maybe two months of the busy season at the Garden Center, pocket a bunch of money and head out west again. They do like their casinos and ghost towns.

Mom puts the bowl on the nightstand, and I walk over and give her a hug. It is something I started doing a bunch of years ago. It was not one of the things that was done in our family. Affection was shown by those words after the beatings, the "we only do this because we love you." My mind is not going down that path right at this point in time; I am holding off all of the past stuff. Instead, I am going to approach this so much differently. I know Mom is happy to see me. She always is. It is Dad that the issue hangs out on, but not today. I get the jump on him right away.

"So, you getting your bets in?" I ask knowing he is a little surprised with the question. I am the one in the family that does not gamble. I know, I have heard it many times before. All of life is a gamble. Perhaps I should say I do not go into casinos and play the odds against myself with the cards or machines. I always figured they had casinos to make money, and I work far too hard for the money I have. Wow, I work far too hard for it. Man I so need to replace some beliefs. If I continue to decide it is hard to make money, than I imagine it will be. Wow, guess I am going to decide it is easy from now on, suddenly smiling bigger than ever, and I am sure my father is wondering what's up.

"I have a few more to bet on still. I won the daily double out at Belmont, so I am playing with their money today. The track conditions are poor so I think the long shots will have a good chance at coming in today," he says as he turns to look at me as I sit down on a stool in the bedroom.

Mom gets up, "Here, sit in this chair," she offers, being the old-fashioned mom/wife who gives up her stuff to the male figures all the time.

"No, I am very comfortable actually, mom, but thank you," I smile and say as I aim my next question at pop. "So, how have you been doing? Have you hit any good ones lately?" The fact that I have asked about the betting he has been doing has him acting like a kid suddenly, because I do not ask or inquire about the racing or betting at all, although he so often tries to bring it up in conversation as we talk.

I know my father has not been feeling well; he looks weaker than usual and has lost a lot of weight over the past bunch of years. Health issues have really been hitting him. He was a large man, a little over 6 feet and weighed about 260 or so, and now he is a man of maybe 230. Weaker or not, you see energy come to his face, and he turns in his chair to face me even more as he gets a confident and proud look and starts to share his best victories over the last few months.

After awhile with me asking another question or two (although it was not necessary; once he started off, there really was no stopping him. He really likes to talk about himself and what he is doing). Suddenly I turn and ask mom, "What is the nicest thing you saw or did out west this time?"

She has to think about this. It is a question she is not really ever asked. It is Dad all things are directed to, yet I know what she will say. Ask either of my sisters, especially my older one Claire; it is almost the standing joke as to what mom will talk about and then it starts.

"Oh, we took some wonderful walks and have seen some great countryside, and the Hot Springs are so nice. I think that is what I like best." Turning and being the good wife she is, she asks, "What do you think, David," and dear old dad is pulled back in to the equation.

He throws in a few other things and then agrees that the things Mother has said are real good too, before Mom finally opens the door to Jim, "So how are things with you? Is real estate going well? It seems from what I read things are really bad and you could see it all the way across the United States as we drove back. So many properties on the market."

"Things are going great for me. I am actually number one in closed transactions in the state for Residential Brokerage so far this year out of almost 600 agents, so I am selling, but this is going to be my last year. I have had enough. I no longer feel that real estate is the best utilization of my skills anymore."

My father and his issues chime in, "So what are you going to do then? You can't just not work."

I look over at my mother and quietly say to my father, "I don't know yet. I just know I no longer want to do real estate and that I no longer desire to live around here." I am not taking the questions at anything other than face value. I am not allowing the past to creep in, and feel he is asking this because…. No, I am seeing this as a bona fide question that he was wondering here and now, no more, no less. The smile creeps back onto my face at the thought. I am actually sitting here and have for a while with him and have no issue with it. However, I do have to admit I am not ready to share with him what I am going to do; I felt it was not time with him yet.

After awhile, he gets up to go to the bathroom, and my mother looks over. I say to her, "I am writing. I have been for about four months already."

"Inspirational?" she asks, as her face lights up as if she has always known it. She certainly has seen me overcome many obstacles in life while maintaining a smile the whole time. She knows from her heart that I have always been meant for this.

I smile and look right into her eyes nodding, as I know she understands why I have not shared it with dad. He has the unique ability to see the things that can go wrong, and perhaps he has come across as being negative when really it is a father's love and concern. I am very open to that possibility today, because it is a perfect day for me.

Looking down at my watch, I see that time has flown by. I have another fun thing I want to sneak into my day, actually many more I believe, I just don't know what the other fun ones are right now.

I stand up as dad makes his way back in and with a hobble kind of walk, he makes his way back over to his chair at the computer. I speak up, "Well, I should get going. I am going to go see Jamie's softball game. It has been really nice seeing you two and I am glad to see you are up and around, Pop."

My mother, as usual, gets up and walks with me to the door. I turn and give her a hug once again, as I am about to part. This may sound like a normal every day thing, but if ever I give her a hug it is as a hello, and not as a goodbye, but I could see in her eyes she was wanting and hoping for one, even though it is not a comfort thing in my family.

"It was great seeing you, mom, you look great," smiling and looking around, for some reason not looking right into her eyes.

"Thanks, you too. And keep up with the writing. Good luck," she says with her heart, not just with her words. She knows we are all meant to do something in life and knows this is for me. Whether it was coaching the little kids in basketball, cheering on my own kids in every day events, or the way I help others at the office, we all have that special connection with the universe on something, where we just know it is what we are supposed to do or that it truly does define us. Writing or inspiring others is mine; no doubt, that is how I connect in this universe. She knows it; I know it.

"Bye, Mom," and I head down the stairs and to my car, feeling so good inside and knowing that I walked away with them feeling good, too. I had so much positive energy around me they had no choice but to end up feeling that way.

"See ya, Ernie," I say as I go by. I almost did not acknowledge him because I was so wrapped up in my thoughts.

"Yup, have all kinds of fun," he says as I go out the door. I grin wide at the common line, but a positive good one.

"You too, my friend," I say and toward the car, I go.

LOOK THEM IN THE EYES SO
THEY CAN SEE YOUR HEART

CHAPTER 13 - MARISSA

I start the car up and think I have no reason to have to do any gratitudes or anything right now, because I am feeling it. I feel great from my head to toe. I look down at my phone, missed two calls, wow, not bad. On a day where I want it to not really ring, it isn't. I see one is from the office and one is Lisa.

Of course, the usual play is call the office to get the important stuff, and then call Lisa to see what's up. As I go to do that I stop myself and tweek my day a little again. I hit send as her name comes up. I will see what my wife wants.

"Hi, hon," I say as she answers the phone. "What's up?"

"Oh, I just wanted to know if you were going to make it to the game or not today. It starts in about 20 minutes. I am heading there now. Jamie forgot her cleats and asked me to drop them off to her," she says and I can hear that she is doing other things at the same time. She is the queen of multi-tasking and doing just one more thing before she takes off.

"Yup, I will be there. May not make the first pitch, but I will be along soon after. I have one more stop to make still,"

I say as I had just decided on the spot to make one more stop. "I just came from seeing my parents, and it was wonderful. It was wild. I feel I need to give all the credit to Eckhart on this one, staying in the now and not allowing the past to creep in made it so easy. I look forward to telling you more about it later on."

"Okay, I will see you there then. Did you get the message I left you at the office?"

"Oh, that was from you? No, I called you first when I saw I had missed one from you." I know the silence is slight disbelief, and I am smiling, thinking of what her face must look like right now. "I love you, and I will see you in a little bit, k?" and hang up.

I then dial another number real fast, as I am driving down the road, and wait for the answer.

"Gwenis dious," I hear from the other end of the phone.

"Gwenis Dious, seniorita," I say to the warm voice on the other end. "Hey, honey, what are you doing?"

"I'm cleaning my room. What are you doing, Daddy?" my youngest daughter says.

"I'm going to go by the house in two minutes. Can you come outside for a minute?"

"Sure, Dad," and then she does her typical hang up without ever saying goodbye. Kind of funny. That bothers some, but I have just always known that is her.

As I make my way to her mom's house, I am thinking to myself, okay, I have been divorced for nine years now, and with my work, I go by the house at least once a day on average, and I have never stopped in just to say hello. I wonder why? If you knew my daughter, you would know she is a warm, lovable, great kid. The type that would bring the schoolmate to the nurse because they said they do not feel well, even if she were having a great time on the playground, she would walk away from all that to help a friend or someone in need.

Can you imagine? I feel as if I am a great dad because I have always picked her up when I am supposed to and take her on nice trips and get her nice things (which she never asks for) yet I have not stopped in just for the sake of letting her know she is important to me.

She is on the screen porch, just kind of standing there waiting for me to show up, and does her oblivious walk down the walkway to the picket fence and opens the gate. She has a look of confusion, almost like she wants to say, "Is every thing okay?" as she comes to the passenger side window. I put the window down, and smiling big, I say, "Hey, honey, hop in for a minute."

"Okay, dad," she says as she opens the door and steps up on the running board. Slams the door shut hard (yup, that's Marissa). "Oops, sorry, Dad," she says, smiling and centers herself in the seat. "What's up?"

"I just thought I would stop in and say hello, pal. What do

you think of that?" I say and see her light up.

"Ahh, cool. So what you doing today? Have lots of appointments?" she asks.

Wow, I think, she knows my world, but do I really know her world? It seems like she is growing up so fast. Seventh grade this year, and oh my goodness, she has gone from little girl to young lady, so wonderful to be able to see and be a part of.

"Had a few this morning, but have tried to just take most of the day off. Went and saw Grandpa and Grandma. They got back a few nights ago."

"I know. Mom told me. She said she saw them when she was driving by going to work the other day," she says as she fidgets in her seat. Just like Daddy, she doesn't do a very good job at sitting still. Personally, I decided it was a trait of a very intelligent person.

After chatting for 10 minutes or so, I say, "Okay, Daddy needs to take off. How great it was to see you; it was special time today wasn't it?" as I smile from ear to ear at her.

"I love you, Daddy," she says as she leans over and gives me a kiss, something she does not do very often. She is very obviously feeling it. Then she turns to open the door.

"You have a great afternoon, okay, pal, and I love you too," as she jumps down and heads to the gate, I can see her feeling the small amount of daddy time was great, special.

In nine years, I have never had the time to stop in because I needed to get to my next thing, whatever that may have been. It is one thing to use an excuse for a week or two, but nine years is a little difficult to overlook. I am going to make sure that I stop in more often now. What I just got out of that time was great, and I saw that she got something out of it, too. I decide that although I could feel sadness for not doing this over the last nine years, instead, I am going to be glad and enjoy the fact and feelings I have because I did stop in today, and look forward to the next time I do this, too.

As I drive away, I tell myself I am going to be a little more alert as I take my ten-minute drive to the softball field. I want to see as many things as I can, good things that I overlook every time I drive this way. It just seems that there are so many beautiful things out here that I have driven by so many times that are popping out to me today. I sure feel like I have connected with another dimension or maybe you could say I am in the middle of a twilight zone.

A STRONG LIGHT BULB
CAN SHINE A LONG WAY

CHAPTER 14 - THE SOFTBALL GAME

Ten minutes later, as I am pulling in to the MCAA field, dust climbs into the air as my tires go over the ground. It is almost as if it is a game to the dust to see which particle can reach highest. Looking in my rear view mirror, I watch the cloud.

I scan the parking lot looking for a light blue convertible Solara. It was a magical day when I found that for her. Thinking about that would have me agree that the universe works with you.

I had called every dealership there was. I had spent a good two hours at my desk at the office dialing dealer after dealer. I had searched the internet like you would not believe and could not find the baby blue. Then, driving back from winning the over 30 championship soccer game in August of 2005, I stopped in at a dealership on a whim. The salesman lets me know that they sell before they ever hit the dealerships or if they do make it, each dealership gets so few that they are gone in the first day or two.

I know, I know. I heard it on basically every call I made during the week. I am a relentless pursuit kind of person that has been failing here. I tell him exactly what I am after and he gives me the salesman talk. Oh yeah, give a top-notch salesman the sales talk, I am thinking. I get the, "Oh, yes, we have one coming in on Monday." He doesn't know what color, but come in and sit down so he can take some information.

I went back to my vehicle and grabbed a business card. I wrote down my cell phone number and told him to please call me right away if it is blue, and we will take care of business.

Getting back in my car, I am still riding high because of the victory we had that day. Five miles down the road while listening to the tunes, I see my phone going off. I turn down the music as fast as I can and answer it. It is that salesman; it is a blue one coming in. I tell him I will give him a deposit right over the phone to hold it, if he can please write it up in the company name on the card and fax me the paperwork, I will take care of all this in the morning.

Now, that was meant to be. That was the universe working in full gear, I am thinking. Or was I letting the universe work? As I spot her car, a smile comes to my face, and I just accept. Either way, it worked perfectly, and I have been falling away from believing in coincidences. There have been just far too many in my life to think I am truly the luckiest person in the world. It has to be that I have attracted the situation.

I am not able to park near her, but get a great space near the entrance. I park and get out. As I step out, I feel as light as a feather today as I walk over toward the backstop and watch the game in process. I scan to try to find Lisa. As I approach the backstop, it looks like Jamie is in the on-deck circle. Perfect, I think, and then think, but of course she is, as I walk to the side of the backstop. A brother and sister my age with a child in the game here are sitting in their chairs watching as well.

"Hey, Jeff, how's it going?" I step to their side so I am not in the way, but only 15 feet from where Jamie will be batting.

"The other team is up by one. Throwing errors in the first is why. They should be able to beat these guys," he says as he keeps his eyes on the game. He has three daughters that play and they all, including him, absolutely live for the game of softball.

"Okay, Jamie, focus hard on that ball. Focus and believe," I say loud enough so she hears. She turns and looks over at me quickly, not making eye contact, but to know exactly where I am.

She steps into the batter's box, and focuses hard on the pitcher and the ball, in it comes and…. Oh, man, that was a lame swing. Her arms swung, but the rest of her body was not playing the game. She is worried about not hitting it rather than hitting it.

"Jamie, make your whole body strong, your whole body, from your legs to your arms. You can do it. You know you can hit her. Now do it," I say from my position behind the backstop.

"Ball," the umpire says as she steps away and looks back at

me. This time I show confidence in my face and body and put my two fists together like I am going to hit it, "Okay, Jamie, make your whole body strong and take care of business," I say this time, as she gets a look of determination and realization that yes, yes, she can do this.

Standing strong with knees bent instead of stiff like sticks, she focuses hard and in it comes. Slam! She hits a rocket over the second baseman's head; she is out of that batter's box and running hard to first. I am all lit up and see a run coming across the plate as I start to make my way to the small set of bleachers that are out in left field where I assume Lisa must be.

I am lit up like you cannot believe, as I make my way. I took my eyes off what Jamie was doing when I hear an "ooohhhh" and a "ya" come from the players and fans. Jamie had almost been picked off first base because she rounded it too far and was not getting back as fast as she should have. I think her head was on Cloud 9. She usually does not hit the ball out of the infield on the fly. I see Lisa glowing at her daughter's hit and yelling to her what a great hit it was. I come up to her and quietly tell her I was behind the backstop giving her confidence. Lisa knows I can make people believe in themselves, and she knows that Jamie has wanted me to help her, but her strong personality can get in the way sometimes. Well, it sure did not today.

I sit up next to her and give the hello kiss again. This is wild; there are at least 15 other parents I am doing this in front of, so it is certainly not the every day thing here. "Hey, honey, how are you? It sure is good to see you," I say as I scoot up next to her, grab her arm, and interlock it with mine.

"So, I decided today, instead of being the quiet guy I usually am and talking to her about what she did well and what she maybe could improve upon back at home when she is defensive, I would speak up here and now today. To heck with the passive help. What do you think of that baby?" I say as I look with a wide smile not showing any teeth, all proud of myself for breaking out of my shell here.

"I am so glad. You know she has been wanting you to cheer her on just like you do Marissa at Marissa's games. She gets so jealous when you yell out and help Marissa and then don't for her," Lisa lets me know.

I look right in her eyes and smile. "I know. It feels good to help her; she is a good kid," I say as I turn and notice she is ready to race off to second base in the stance I taught her, even though the coach told her to do it another way. I never really understood why he said that, but even at 12, Jamie knows the advantage of what I showed her and is using it.

As the afternoon goes on, Jamie is playing second base and she had booted a ball hit to her and wasn't taking it well. She was kicking the dirt all mad at herself. I look over at Lisa and say, "Oh no, the real Jamie is coming to the surface. I think I need to give her a little pep talk between innings. What do you say?" smiling big as I look her in the eyes.

Lisa's eyes get big and she is nodding, "Yes, good idea. She needs to learn to be able to control her emotions. She is getting better, but still has a ways to go."

I nod in agreement as I am sure she is also reminiscing

about her games a few years ago where she would be pitching and have a meltdown, and I do mean a meltdown. She would simply stand on the mound and stare after she had walked a batter. I pitied anyone who tried to yell words of encouragement to her. She would give you the dirtiest look you have ever seen. The players, coaches, fans, everyone would be waiting for her to pitch again, and she wouldn't. She would just stand there with a look on her face.

She is a very talented player in all sports, and has the absolute highest expectations of herself, so if she falls back into human status and does something wrong (like an error) she simply cannot deal with it.

About five minutes later, Jamie is running off the field after the third out and you can see that look of disgust for booting the ball. She had another hit to her and she was able to get the girl out at first base, but she did not handle the ball cleanly.

I walk to the chain link fence, and look for her in the dugout. I am actually about 15 feet from the dugout, so when I finally do get her attention, I will be able to speak to her privately.

Making eye contact with her, and motioning her to come over, she does. She has her hat in her hand and almost stomps. When she gets there, the first words out of her mouth are, "I can't do anything right out there."

Smiling and making direct eye contact with her, "Jamie, that was a really nice hit. That felt real good, huh?"

I watch her face start to light up. I figure this is a shifter for her; give her that nice thought to shift the negative feelings and beliefs that she has suddenly taken on. Then I see it start to fade back toward what it was. "Jamie, I need you to take a deep breath, first through you mouth, and slowly let it out, and then take a deep breath through your nose, and blow it out your mouth."

After she does this (cleansing her body and shifting her thoughts at the same time), I lean forward grabbing the chain link fence with both hands and quietly say, "Secret."

"Jamie, listen to what you told me when you came over: 'I can't do anything right out there.' You need to change that. When the batter is up, I want you focused and ready and say to yourself, hit it to me. Then focus and have a look of determination that you are so good at. I have always been amazed how you can get and do anything when you are properly focused, and I know that right now you are. That hit proved it."

I turn to walk away. Rome was not built in a day. I feel I did as much damage control as I could get away with at this point in time. I do believe she has shifted enough to be able to snap out of it. Then suddenly I turn back and speak, "Jamie, your team needs you to be upbeat. You are a leader and they need to believe in themselves right now if you are to win. You are that person who can change it for the team," I am nodding my head as I do this and as I walk away. I also see her slowly walk back toward the dugout thinking about what I have said.

Back over on the bench, Lisa and I chat on this and watch

her behavior with surprise. Jamie actually is cheering on her teammates like she never has before, and as they rally and score some runs, she looks over at us with this big smile of accomplishment, as if she is the reason for the rally. I sit and actually wonder a small amount on that, if she ended up truly believing what I had said, than yes she was able to connect to the universe and bring about the rally. She could have created the vibrational energy necessary to make that happen.

The team ended up doing much better and as we got near the end of the game, my normal behavior crept in. Coming into the last inning, I turn to Lisa and say, "You want me to go home and get supper going?"

"You can if you want," knowing that it is so unusual for me to stay for an entire game. I am always off to the next thing so quickly all the time, "But I would rather you stay here and watch the rest of the game with me. But if you prefer you can go," she adds.

I sit and ponder to myself. One day, I can do this, she is right. I feel uncomfortable here now, feeling I need to get supper made, but it is such a rare occasion that I remain, even if the score is tied and the game is high excitement. I must focus, relax and tell myself how wonderful it is simply being here with the woman I love out in this open air. The funny thing is, if this were my last day on earth and I was asked what I would want to do or whom I would want to be with, she is the one. Of course, I would have to sneak in some time with my two daughters Marissa and Cassi, as well. I lean back and smile and tell her, "Supper can wait, as long as I get to be here with you." All along I am thinking to myself who is this person that is saying these things and loving the person at the same time?

DECIDE SIMPLE THINGS ARE
SPECIAL, AND THEY WILL BE

CHAPTER 15 - SUPPER TIME

"See you in a little bit, honey," as I walk toward my car and Lisa waits for the team to have its meeting before Jamie is able to go. I get in my car and look down at my phone. Two more missed calls. Hmm not bad, as I reach to hit the backdoor line to get the messages, start the car up, buckle and suddenly decide I will wait until I am out on the road and then call, that not everything needs to be done instantly. The small snafus that I have are melting away today, because I am observing the behavior that I would usually support with all kinds of reasons as to why I am this way and why it is good or better.

As I pull out on the road, and am comfortably moving along, I call in to get my messages. The usual thing to do is immediately get back to these people. I kind of do, by calling them and letting them know I will be on their want/need first thing in the morning and I will give them a call by mid-morning at the latest. Jim, who does everything instantly, pushes off the return calls to a time that is more comfortable instead!

Hanging up, I realize I am actually freaking myself out a little bit, but also have been able to put aside my feelings that I must do these things right away. I am becoming conscious of how I was creating the mentality that I "had to" get back to them right away or something bad would happen. If something bad did not really happen, I would at least have created something bad in my head, to be able to support my irrational behavior. My brain is quite something really, to be able to do all this. However, the important thing to remember is that on this one very special day, I decided that bad things would not happen on anything, only good things, and by golly, that is what has happened.

Pulling in the driveway, I am trying to think how else I can add a little secret into my day. What else can I do that would be special and wonderful or at least something that pushes me out of my comfort zone? Well, maybe not out of the comfort zone but something that would take me off autopilot.

I go inside and look in the fridge to see what was taken down for supper tonight. I see it is steak tips, yum yum, and hunt down the veggies. Within five minutes, I have gotten food moved forward and have the veggies on the stove ready to be turned on. I decide the starch will be microwaved potatoes tonight. I get the potatoes cleaned up and then hear the garage door open. Lisa is home with Jamie. 6:35. It is not all that late; we can be eating by 7:00, I say to myself when she comes through the door.

"Hey, Lisa, I was just thinking how much I would enjoy a nice relaxing walk around the block, not a power walk, just a nice relaxing, let's enjoy the open air walk. What do you say?"

"I want to come too," Jamie says almost instantly. It is as

if she could feel the joy that was in my voice of how nice it would be and fed off it.

"You need to get in the shower and get to your homework, Jamie," Lisa lets her know right away. "You have a lot to do, you said, and you have been staying up way too late."

I stand there trying to think of some way to make it special to Jamie and I'm hopeful that she will accept this; history says she will be really upset and react harshly. How is it humanly possible to get the reaction to be different as we hear the grumbling begin about how she never gets to do any fun stuff. Wow, do you hear that? There is so much positive energy around that, a simple walk is thrown in the category of "fun stuff." I am smiling to myself at that one and decide I am going to keep the good energy flowing rather than falling into the defensive trap that has been laid out.

"Great game today, Jamie," I yell up the stairs. "That was an awesome hit, and I look forward to talking to you about the game out on the screen porch after supper."

Yes, the back porch, our relaxation ground. A real nice swing set up, comfy chairs, a small table and a big table to be able to enjoy supper out there if we desire. Hmm, can't think of that happening as often as it should; we will have to change that. I turn to Lisa, smiling and feeling like I have achieved a huge victory with Jamie and hopeful of sliding out of the home before the weather on that one changes. "You ready, hon?" I ask as I am grinning ear to ear.

"Just one minute, I will be right with you. I just need to…," she is saying as she is walking up the stairs. I'm not sure exactly what she is saying, but I did catch the part about one more minute so I grab my sneakers and put them on. Looks kind of neat, I think, nice suit and a pair of Nikes. Now that is an ad, I think, as I stand up and look down at my feet. Lisa will think I look funny and the care bus for old Jimbo will be empty. I just know it will be a nice walk with the one I love, so the look of my outfit just doesn't come into play for me.

Standing out in the driveway, I wait for Lisa to come out. Here she comes spouting right away, "Sorry, I had to...," she starts but I cut her off.

"Relax, slow down, dude. I am so relaxed and this is going to be such a nice walk. If ever there was an evening that we pictured in our mind as to what it would be like in this neighborhood this is it. Look at the sun going down, a beautiful view. The birds are chirping away, the pansies are smiling up at us there, and the trees with the new year's leaves are out strong now. Dude, this is life at the fullest. It is and has been here all the time. Do you understand how we look past that every single day and put other much less important stuff into our lives and then mistakenly decide those things are what is important?" I say.

"Lisa, this has been the most incredible day of my life. You have no idea, and actually, I had no idea. Not allowing my normal thought process to enter into the day and by moving toward every good feeling I had more and more. I truly believed that no matter what, everything would turnout perfectly. It made my day," I share as I stare at the ground going over it in my head.

I look up and at her, "I have so many things I want to share as to how my day went and how it was perfect because I decided it would be that way and would not allow anything to change that. I decided for just today, I could handle doing that, and I had to look and listen to myself many times to change my normal thought process and patterned behavior. By doing that, I had what has been one of the greatest days of my life, so I ask, why would I not do all this again?"

I stop and face her, making her stop, too. "Lisa, this is where it is so important for me to let the secret grow inside me. It would be so easy to say as much as I want to keep it all warm and fuzzy, real life is out there and tomorrow I have blah blah blah...."

I kick the ground a little and then look up at her sternly, "Instead, to truly live *The Secret,* I need to tell myself that everything will work out perfectly, that it will be one of the greatest days of my life. I just know that I will be able to see my patterned behavior creep back in, be able to identify it, and change it before I slip and fall into it. I may fall into small holes, but as soon as I start to fall in, I will see and understand the behavior that had me falling in and stop it. I will also be able to avoid all the big holes out there. Today for some reason I was able to see that what people do is jump feet first into the holes almost like mind-controlled robots. Then while they are down in the hole they not only jumped into, but dug, then complain of being in that hole."

"Today I saw and understood myself more than I ever have before. I create my own holes, jump in them and keep myself firmly planted in them. Now get this, honey. I, at the same time, if asked about why I am in the hole I just dug, would respond subconsciously and explain that it is not my fault. I would be able to deflect all responsibility to others. Even if you saw me digging the hole and jumping in, my subconscious would explain it isn't my fault. And if you give me too much trouble about the behavior, I might even become aggressive to try to help protect my behavior." I smile at this and feel how ridiculous a statement it is, yet it is truly how we are. The inner being will really go to great lengths to protect itself. Imagine if we are able to identify this in our everyday walk through life. We truly could help create a much better life for ourselves. I don't want to go through life as an unconscious being having auto-responders rule my life. I want to take back the control and allow myself to grow and enjoy life the way it should be.

I start walking again and quietly say, "We need to help each other on this. You read *The Secret* and Lori has. We have to get the kids too or maybe we should be reading it to them. If we surround ourselves with positive energy, behavior and beliefs, life cannot help itself but get better. We need to think of things we can do so we all live life fuller and better," I say.

Lisa is walking at a relaxed pace and you can tell the wheels are turning upstairs. She is not a passive woman, but a very assertive one who has desire to improve the quality of life for all. She has a great heart, and always wants to fix everything for everybody. "What if I got little books for all of us to write down five things we are grateful for each day?" she quietly says, as you can tell she is still in deep thought. "And I bet you I could get Elliot to read the book," she adds as she is still thinking. "And maybe now is the time I should tell you I bought three Vision Books online from Jack Canfield (co-author of Chicken Soup for the Soul). I thought we could each do one here at night, you, me, and Elliot. Also, remember that thing I told you? You know, the thing I wanted to go to with you? Jack Canfield is doing that workshop about the power of attraction. I really feel like we are supposed to go," she says looking straight at me.

I am nodding my head. It is so nice creating energy together toward a common goal and knowing that we can truly help our kids have a higher quality of life and achieve so much more for themselves if we not only tell them to believe in themselves, but show how we live and believe in that same manner.

"Okay, Lisa, listen to this. You know how we have this great life and we look at others and know how they too can so easily, if they just understood or did this or that or believed. How we can look at them and know that they are what are holding themselves back. That you get and are what you are by believing that is where you should be," I blurt out.

"Well, what if all these other people who achieved so much more than us, looked at us, and said the exact same thing?" my mouth almost hanging open as if I am saying, duh, Jim, to myself. "What if a bunch of them joined together and came up with a simple success formula and said and explained how easy it is to achieve what they do?" Now I am looking right at her with, do you get it written all over my face. "Lisa, that is what *The Secret* is. They have done this for us and most of the population will not believe it or be able to do it. Not us. We are going to break through. They are telling us how and let's do it. Let us be the few that can actually do it," I state firmly.

"We are very intelligent beings; we need to be able to realize that the average human being cannot make this breakthrough because they do not believe. I feel that is the number one stopping block. Just as those below what we achieve don't believe they can, or the agents at the office who never had the sales we had when we know they all can do it, but they stop themselves. They don't believe they can, so therefore they can't," I say. I'm realizing how we can, we truly can, if we believe. "If one believes, they start acting in a different way that brings about the success instead of continuing with their current behavior that was supportive of the previous production. Really, it is that simple. We need to add and use the principles they have written out."

"Think of it, Lisa. Most people will say I can't, you don't understand, or whatever other reason their Ego needs to give to support where exactly they are in life. The 24 people in the book who have done this, each with a story of how they overcame odds or obstacles like we would never believe, are saying, hello, we all did it and this is how." I share with so much enthusiasm because I believe I am breaking through already by allowing myself to understand and realize my own human behavior pattern.

Suddenly I hear something hit the ground. I look down. It is Lisa's ear; I talked it off. I reach over pick it up and hand it to her. "Sorry about that, I have been talking this whole time I have not allowed you to say anything. Please share further," I ask.

"No, I think that," she starts and I interrupt right away.

"You said no. What were you saying no to?" I ask.

She is looking puzzled and starts off, "No, I didn't," and then you see her questioning herself because she does realize she just said it again. "Or did I? Hmm I don't know why," she says.

"We need to create yeses in our life, only yeses," I say.

"Well, what I was going to say is, yes, I do believe we can, and this is what I love the most. How we talk and dream like this. I just love that," and she turns to me and says, "You can do anything, Jim, I know that and have always believed that."

"Thanks, honey, and I so want to talk on this further. Can we go to bed early tonight so we can chat? Just you and me, for awhile, and see if we can come up with a plan together?" I ask as I look at her as we walk back up the driveway. It was a beautiful mile walk that really had no distance to it; we never once had any thought about what we were doing; we simply were caught up in the beauty of potential. If our minds are going to float off, we might as well have them float toward beauty, and we did.

"We can try," she says as she looks at me and realizes that she gave the wrong answer. Her answer states that she does not believe we will be able to. Then she starts off again, "I can tell Jamie she needs to be in bed by 9, actually in her room, not doing other things, and as long as you are okay with early being by 9:15, yes," she adds.

This is one of those areas where Lisa and I are so different. I am a person who needs his sleep. In my perfect world (the perfect world I created and believed in my head), I would be asleep by 9:15. Looking at her as I open the door going from the garage to the house, I smile and say, "Yes, that sounds perfect."

WHAT BELIEFS ARE YOU GOING TO CHANGE?

1)

2)

3)

4)

5)

FOCUS ON EVERYTHING YOU HAVE DECIDED IS GOOD

CHAPTER 16 - THE SCREEN PORCH

Jamie was out of the shower when we got back, a record for her, and supper went off smoothly and easily. Lisa and I were both so at ease, the energy that was in the house was low key and relaxed.

It was amazing how nice it was sitting and enjoying supper together; it was quiet and almost euphoric. We were all happy and smiling and enjoying the meal, a very simple thing really. Once done, no one hopped up from the table; it was as if we were in this zone and didn't want to leave it. Jamie ended up laying on the bench that she sits on at the table, and Lisa sat back and didn't move; she would look toward the piece of steak on the plate now and then and sneak a small piece off the end, almost as if it was giving her an excuse to remain a little longer.

Me, I also sat back and observed our behavior, mine included. I felt these same feelings, instead of wanting to shove it into overdrive and get the next thing done so we could end the day and pretend we were relaxing. We were instead enjoying the right here, right now.

I am going over all the wonderful things that happened in

my head (or that I created or brought into my universe today consciously), all the wonderful things that created this point in time. In my deep thoughts, I am realizing that usually this is a more stressful time of the night as I try to get the kids off the computer and to their homework. I also realize that this is when I am going through my day and over the crap that happened.

Whether I want to admit it or not (and of course I do not), I usually find the worst things that occurred in my day and share it with Lisa. All I am doing, even though I consider myself such an upbeat guy, is putting negative energy into the air. I am sending out a vibration that connects and creates more of this exact same energy due to the power of attraction with all that is around me. Now, if you ever tried to tell me I created it, I would have cursed you and let you know you have no idea what you are talking about. You try to find someone more upbeat and full of life than me! I would have attacked you and your own behavior and probably thrown in something like, who the heck are you to tell me?

I stop myself from going down this road in my mind; this is my Secret day, and it is not over yet. Instead, I focus on all the great energy that is around me right now and decide to show even further how it works.

"Ok, Jamie," I look down at her because she is lying on the bench, "Time to get to your homework my friend," smiling and knowing she understands.

She starts to sit up, her body slumping some, but yet you can still tell, full of energy, "I know." She starts to smile as she is grabbing her plate to put it in the dishwasher, "I was just so relaxed, I didn't want to get up," she says. When I notice she did not take her silverware, "Hey, Jamie, get back here and grab the silverware. You always do that, you grab your plate and nothing else and we end up having to clean up after you. How fair is that?"

Oh my, aren't you feeling all kinds of uncomfortable feelings on the inside right now? Weren't you feeling good and at ease reading about the wonderful relaxing time and then suddenly I made a nothing thing a major issue and destroyed all I had built. If you tried to tell me I was destroying the atmosphere that was all around me, I would have told you it had nothing to do with me. If she could simply pick up her silverware, the whole situation never would have happened. Think to yourself, though, if not the silverware, would my mind have found something else to pick up on instead? Well, rest easy, the second part never came. After Jamie picked up her plate, I simply smiled as I saw the silverware on the table still. That silly girl, she so often leaves them there, but she is very good at getting her plate.

I look over at Lisa as she puts her hands on her tummy rubbing it gently, "That was so good, I feel like I could eat more and more, but know I shouldn't," she says as she has a very content look on her face.

"I understand," I say. "Believe me, I understand," as I get up and walk to the dishwasher with my plate and start the clean up routine.

For the next ten minutes, we clean up, and even though it

takes only ten minutes, what usually seems like a pain-in-the-butt chore is actually quite relaxing and easy. It is the same teamwork we usually use, me putting things away and Lisa doing clean up, yet the atmosphere is so much different today. Even Jamie doing her homework is going well; she would usually be at the computer doing instant messaging (while of course saying she isn't) while she does her homework there, but tonight, she is up at the center counter spread out and really focusing on getting it done. Yet, I also wonder if she subconsciously wants to be closer to us because the air is so wonderful around us.

Looking at Lisa, it is almost like she felt me looking and she turns and makes eye contact, I simply say, "Back porch?"

"Yeah, you going to have something to drink?" she asks.

"I sure am. It is one of those nights I know a glass of wine is going to taste so good and I am going to go get one of my nice bottles that I save." Smiling, thinking how I often wonder, and how she is poking at me all the time asking, what am I saving them for? She says I get them to enjoy them and then never feel the occasion is special enough to ever break one open. "I'll be back," I say as I head to the basement to look over my good bottles and I hear her getting out a shaker to mix herself up something special.

Sooner than usual, I come upstairs with a nice bottle of Australian Shiraz with this look of great satisfaction on my face, for two reasons really. One being it did not take me very long to chose, and the second being I am allowing myself to enjoy one of my good bottles.

A few minutes later we are heading out to the back porch, and I can see Jamie turn her head and look up a little wanting to join us, but knowing she needs to get her homework done. We sit in our normal spots, with a small table between our chairs and able to see each other by a very small simple slight turn of our heads.

"What a day today," I say nodding my head with satisfaction. "I have tried to figure out if I attracted all this beauty into my life today or simply saw what was always here. Or did I just not allow myself to focus on any of the crap that I guess I have mostly created with my mind?" I say as I am looking off up into space as if the answer is written up there and I am supposed to see it.

"Did you notice how relaxing and at ease supper was and how easily Jamie went about doing her homework? We didn't fight with her on it and she didn't with us. It was as if the energy that surrounded the area tonight would not allow any of the negative energy to creep in," I share with a semi profound look on my face.

"Negative attracts negative, positive attracts positive. Usually we are expecting a fight for her to do it, and tonight, we did not expect it, and we did not get one. Is it us?" I ask as I look at her with a furrowed brow. "Her or all us together?"

"I almost want to say, why can't we have this every day? And I feel the answer is because we do not believe we can." Eyes wide, as if, duh, if we don't believe it how could it possibly happen? "What are your thoughts?" I ask.

"I don't know. I am just living in the moment right now. This is what I always envisioned when I thought of us together," she says as she tilts her head back and takes a deep cleansing breath. Looking at her, I smile; she looks so at ease, so relaxed, so comfortable. Wow, is all I can think.

I turn my head back to the sky and look out on it. "You're right. Me too. It has always been here for us to have it this way; it is like it was there for the taking, put into our laps, and we just never picked it up, but today we did. We put too much focus in what we do not want to happen, but today we didn't do that; we focused on what we wanted, and it found us," I say smiling and looking back over at her staying in the moment.

I reach out and take a sip of my wine. A good choice it was, or is it the moment? Who knows? I don't have to figure that out. I am simply here to enjoy what is in front of me, being this beautiful home, and it has been in front of me for five years now, yet for some reason, I feel like even though I was not here very much today, I have enjoyed it (or at least felt it) more today than ever. Sure we have had some very wonderful times here, but never as relaxed as what we are feeling today. Feels like it is a gift, yet if it is a gift, it is a gift I gave myself today. I wonder as I sit there if she is looking at me, as I am nodding my head in agreement, that yes, I gave myself a gift.

I look over at her and have so much desire to share, but just sum it up, "You know, I got such fulfillment out of the day today by connecting with the universe in only positive energy. Many times I almost slipped, but when I did I quickly corrected myself, and I only believed good things would come no matter what. I allowed myself to enjoy so many things that I want to each day. For some reason, and I have not been able to come up with reasons as to why I had not done things I have wanted to, not just for days or weeks, but sometimes years on things I had done today. I did things that made me feel good, and I did not allow anything to change me feeling that way," I share as I turn back in my chair and look up at the sky. "I connected and it felt good; it is kind of like in the Bible or in church where they say God is always there, it is us who are not. This has certainly been a wild day."

Suddenly my cell phone is going off. I look at my watch. 8:38. Usually, I would jump right up to get it and get it back to whomever right away. I look over at Lisa and smile, "I think that can wait until the morning, how about you?" I ask.

"That's up to you. Whatever makes you more comfortable," she says as she is so relaxed and at ease; it feels so good and nice to look over and see her this way.

I sit back and relax, "Well, I believe the call will or could be whatever I decide to create in my own mind, and today it has been different, and tonight I decide that the call is one that is no big deal and can wait until the morning."

After another 10 to 15 minutes of just being, Jamie comes out and hugs her mom. I sit there thinking how nice that is and smile. Then suddenly I get the biggest shock of my entire day; she comes over and leans down hugging me, and says, "I am glad you're my step dad."

"Why thank you very much," I say with a warmth I was unaware I was capable of with an ear-to-ear grin. "That was very nice of you. I really appreciate that. I am glad you are my step daughter."

In my head, I am thinking of how she has never ever said that even though I have been in her life for nine years. Lisa and I always felt that the kids do not show me any affection because they feel like they would be selling out their true father. I am thinking perhaps we/I am partially to blame. Perhaps I have not allowed this to happen in the last nine years. Oh my, the wonderful things that have found me and that I have found today. How can I possibly follow up a day like this, I am asking myself, when I catch myself and say out loud to try to cover it and directly to Lisa, "My life gets better and better every single day. It is wonderful to have it increase and improve every day," I blurt out as I look at her with my "yeah" look. I feel good, I got an affirmation in to cover my tracks, my life can get better and better each and every day if I let it.

"So you ready to go up, honey?" I say. I know we both feel in a daze and could just sit out here and eventually watch the sunrise. Leaning towards her I say, "I feel like it is going to be so nice and relaxing up in our beautiful room, sitting back against the headboard with the pillows all fluffed up, and reminiscing about the day. Or we could just enjoy the here and now," I say as I slowly start to get up thinking of another little change I can put in my day before it comes to a close.

WHAT CAN YOU DO TO MAKE
AN AVERAGE SITUATION SPECIAL?

1)

2)

3)

4)

5)

ANOTHER PERFECT DAY :)

CHAPTER 17 - TIME FOR BED

Walking back into the house, the usual routine would be Lisa picking up the final things downstairs, making sure the garage door is closed, front door locked, dishwasher going, counter cleaned off, and a basic scan of the downstairs to make sure all is in order so she feels at ease when she starts her next day. My usual routine would be to go upstairs, brush my teeth, get in bed and wonder when she is ever going to come to bed.

Tonight once again it is different. As I finish loading the last couple dishes and get the dishwasher going, she comes in and says, "I'll take care of that," and almost seems like I have taken something that is hers and she feels wrong me having it.

"I am more than happy to take care of this; you can go spend a few minutes with Jamie, or get yourself ready for bed. I'll be up in a few minutes," I say as I am running this through my mind wondering why this is basically the first time I have done this. On the surface, it seems it will be a few minutes closer to when we will get to the last relaxing part of our day.

Lisa is standing there almost like she should not let me do what is rightfully hers; it is like she is not allowing me to and I feel the smile growing on my face again. She is heading toward the garage to check that door and to make sure the dog is set for the night. I walk around the counter and put my hands on her hips and look down into her eyes, "Honey, I feel the greatest use of Lisa right now is to spend a few special minutes with your daughter upstairs. I will have this done in two minutes and meet you upstairs in a little bit, okay," I say, as I can see she is still slightly struggling with this.

"Are you sure?" she says, as she is looking deep into my eyes to make sure that this is the real reason, and then finishes her sentence with, "Thanks I appreciate that." Funny how we do not allow things in our life; she wasn't allowing me to help her.

After she goes up, and I finish the small routine, I stand in the kitchen and look around. Sixteen plus hours ago, I got up and started this day. I had decided to change my mindset for one simple day. Usually, I would be exhausted by this time of the night, especially after getting up so early, but I do not feel that way. I feel quite good, content. It was an effort today, but the effort was so worthwhile, the connections I made with my world were quite something. It is like the universe has been sitting patiently waiting for me to interact with it in an even more positive manner than I have been and it responded and did its part. It kind of feels like the universe has so wanted me to be upbeat beyond my normality and was responding in every way it could. It is a rare thing that occurs. All the rest of the universe must have heard about what I was doing and all the positive behavior that came flooding into my life today from all over. It is like the universe lives and seeks out someone acting like I was each day, so that it can show how incredible life can be if you allow it. All it took was mental discipline and allowing me to keep an eye on myself.

Our own minds are where we decide it cannot be that way; it must be so frustrating to the universe to sit and watch this as it wants to show us how incredible life can be when we in our own minds decide, no it cannot be that way. What if this happens, or what if that happens? Better yet, I better not act or be all happy go lucky because so and so may not like that. To heck with that stuff, I feel. The greater I decide my life will be, the greater it WILL be.

I make my way over to the stairs to head up; I check the door to make sure it is locked and look out onto the front yard. It is so nice out there. I open the door, go out onto the front porch, and look out over the yard. It looks so nice. We have such a beautiful home.

I put my hands on the railing and scan the yard and all the shrubs and trees that make up such a beautiful landscape here. I am wondering, am I delaying the end of the third greatest day of my life (getting married to Lisa and the kids' birth still beat it)? I turn and go back in, lock the door, and head up the stairs.

Once at the top, I yell in to Jamie to my right, "Nice game today, Jamie, I am so glad I went and especially got to see that hit."

"Night, Jim, and thanks for coming," she says as I see

her mom sitting on the bed talking to her, and the atmosphere seems so peaceful; somehow, we knew there would be no issue with her going to bed tonight.

After brushing my teeth, I make my way to the bed; suddenly it is not like I am feeling tired, but yet a feeling of oh my, that bed is going to feel so good. I realize that usually I would be calculating out in my mind, right here, right now, how many hours of sleep I would be getting (even though I do not set my alarm). Based on that, I decide right on the spot whether it would enough and predetermine how my day is going to be tomorrow based upon that data. How wild is that, as I am suddenly thinking how silly that is? If my hours would come up between seven and eight, I would say that will be okay; instead of deciding that I am going to sleep so well and tomorrow is going to be such a wonderful day. Another little change I can put on the end of my day to make the next one even more glorious.

Lisa walks in the room and turns right into the bathroom to finish her routine; she is doing it slightly different tonight. There is a bounce in her step rather than a rush, you know, the oh my goodness, I need to get to bed because he has been waiting and he likes to get his sleep so I better hurry. She comes out, then goes into the walk-in closet, and comes out wearing a little something she has not worn in awhile. I smile as I see her in it; she looks gorgeous. "Wow, you look great honey. Good choice," I say thinking she hasn't put that on in at least a year, but tonight she feels great inside and somehow knew this was appropriate instead of the same old nightshirt.

She gets in bed, pulls the covers over her body, and leans

over and gives me a kiss. She remains propped up on her arm looking at me. "I love you," she says, as she takes her propped up arm and lets it slide down, so she is laying her head on the bed.

I want to share with her all the things that happened today, and then suddenly realize that this would not be the best thing to do. I have shared many of these things today, but to truly live in the here and now moment, that is not the best thing. I also slide down, throwing a couple of the pillows on the floor that had propped me up and put my left arm out for her to lay her head on my chest. No words needed to be said; it was as if we were a well-oiled machine on that. The best way to share my day would be to live it the same way tomorrow. It does not matter what it is I do or don't do; it is how I decide it is or will be. I simply need to decide it will all be perfect no matter what.

"Honey, what was the greatest thing that happened in your day today?" I suddenly ask, quietly knowing that I was going to end the night on the most positive note possible.

"Just being with you," she says as she snuggles her head a little.

"Thanks, and being with you made it wonderful for me, too," I share as I slide into the now and feel how nice it is, her head gently laying on my chest and feeling her so close. "I am sure loving being here right this minute with you, but I really must say, I so look forward to tomorrow."

"Sleep well, honey, and thank you for being in my life."

OUTSTANDING BOOKS THAT HAVE INSPIRED MY THINKING:

Byrne, Rhonda. The Secret. Atria Books/BeyondWords: Nov. 28, 2006.

Gladwell, Malcolm. Blink: The Power of Thinking Without Thinking. Little, Brown and Company; 1 ed. Jan. 11, 2005.

Haanel, Charles F. The Master Key System. Filiquarian Publishing, LLC.: July 12, 2007.

Hicks, Esther. The Law of Attraction: The Basics of the Teachings of Abraham. Hay House; 1 ed.: Sep. 25, 2006.

Hill, Napoleon. Think and Grow Rich. Ballantine Books (May 12, 1987)

Kelly-Gangi, Carol. The Dalai Lama: His Essential Wisdom. Barnes & Noble Books: Jan. 1, 2007.

Mandino, Og. The Choice. Bantam: Mar. 1, 1986

Mandino, Og. The Greatest Salesman in the World. Bantam: Jan. 1, 1983.

Tolle, Eckhart. The Power of Now: A Guide to Spiritual Enrichment. New World Library; 1 ed.: Sep. 27, 1999.

Tolle, Eckhart. A New Earth: Awakening to Your Life's Purpose. Dutton Adult: Oct. 11, 2005.

Vitale, Joe. The Key: The Missing Secret for Attracting Anything You Want. Wiley: Oct. 19, 2007.

Wattles, Wallace D. The Science of Getting Rich. Top of the Mountain Publishing; 13 ed.: Jan. 2002.

GO OUT INTO THE WORLD TOMORROW
AND ONLY SEE THE BEAUTIFUL THINGS,
DO NOT SEE, ACKNOWLEDGE, OR BE A
PART OF ANYTHING BUT THE BEAUTY.

Intermedia Publishing Group

Publishing That Works For You

Do you need a speaker?

Do you want James Goddard to speak to your group or event? Then contact Larry Davis at: (623) 337-8710 or email: ldavis@intermediapr.com or use the contact form at: www.intermediapr.com.

Whether you want to purchase bulk copies of *Freedom For A Day* or buy another book for a friend, get it now at: www.imprbooks.com.

If you have a book that you would like to publish, contact Terry Whalin, Publisher, at Intermedia Publishing Group, (623) 337-8710 or email: twhalin@intermediapub.com or use the contact form at: www.intermediapub.com.